KEES V

IMMIGRANT GONE
to Heaven

Dutch Polder to Canada's Frontiers

Author's Field Camp on Mandarte Island

FriesenPress

Suite 300 - 990 Fort St
Victoria, BC, V8V 3K2
Canada

www.friesenpress.com

Copyright © 2021 by Kees Vermeer
First Edition — 2021

Edited by Rebecca A. Vermeer

All rights reserved.

No part of this publication may be reproduced in any form, or by any means, electronic or mechanical, including photocopying, recording, or any information browsing, storage, or retrieval system, without permission in writing from FriesenPress.

Front Cover Photo Caption
Kees (front) and companion Roy resting on manual speeder along the railroad track near Lakelse Lake between Terrace and Kitimat, British Columbia, Canada, 1955.

Back Cover Photo Caption
Field Camp on Triangle Island, BC, 1975. (Photo Credit for the Tufted Puffin: Adobe Stock 101493283)

ISBN
978-1-5255-6436-9 (Hardcover)
978-1-5255-6437-6 (Paperback)
978-1-5255-6438-3 (eBook)

1. BIOGRAPHY & AUTOBIOGRAPHY, PERSONAL MEMOIRS

Distributed to the trade by The Ingram Book Company

"*Immigrant Gone to Heaven* is a remarkable book. It grips the reader from the moment the author joins an Emigration Training Centre in the Biesbosch region of the Netherlands with the goal of moving to Canada. We follow his experiences as he lands in Canada and works his way up from farm-hand to obtaining a doctorate in Zoology. The section of the book detailing his explorations in ornithology are as fascinating as the stories of immigration and the memories of World War II. The book takes the reader on a riveting journey of exploration in many facets of social history and science as viewed through the lens of an inquisitive and always optimistic upbeat man. I strongly recommend this book to anyone interested in learning more about World War II, immigration, bird behavior or even just in how a life's journey can unfold with all its unexpected twists and turns."

—Tom Bijvoet, Publisher, DUTCH the Magazine – Maandblad de krant

"Brimming with charming personal anecdotes and fascinating ornithological research in equal measure, Kees Vermeer's *Immigrant Gone to Heaven* paints a vivid picture of an adventurous and fearless life. Vermeer's curiosity and insight into the natural world are evident from his descriptions of childhood nest-hunting in the Dutch polder, to his pioneering work with seabirds on British Columbia's windswept Triangle Island. His stories of everyday life under Nazi occupation are enthralling in their own right. Naturalists, scientists and history buffs alike will enjoy this book."

—Annie McLeod, Editor of Nature Saskatchewan's Blue Jay.

This story is dedicated to my wife Rebecca, who accepted many of life's challenges in Canada and the Philippines, and to my daughter Lotus, who continues on the path of conservation in the United States of America.

Table of Contents

Introduction ix

PART I
Life as an Immigrant 1

Biesbosch—My Last Station 3
On the Move to Canada 9
From the Farm to Alpine Meadows 19
My Salvation Army Home 23
Living in a Boxcar 29
Student Life and Journey to Holland 35
Finding my Niche 41
Mandarte Island 47
Goodbye MSc, Hello PhD 53
Finishing my PhD 59
Wedding at Lunch Break 63

PART II
Life of an Ornithologist 67

Roaming the Dutch Polder 69
First Years of Marriage 77
Pleas for Protection of Fish-eating Bird Colonies 87
Pursuing the Trail of Pesticides and Mercury in Aquatic Birds 95
Back to Seabirds in British Columbia 107
Seabird Studies and Tragedy on Triangle Island 115

Rhinoceros Auklet Fish Sampling Expeditions 123
Cassin's Auklets as Monitors of Zooplankton and Climate Change 129
Storm-petrels in Haida Gwaii 135
Strait of Georgia and other Marine Ecosystems 141
References 155

PART III
Reminiscences of Youth and World War II 163

Early Years in Noordeloos 165
Our Family Adapts to the German Occupation 177
The Last Stretch 187
Memories of the Liberation of Gorinchem 189

PART IV
Tributes to Kees and Rebecca A. Vermeer 193

Kees Vermeer: Scientist and Conservationist 197
Edward Grey Institute of Field Ornithology 205
Early Days: Clutch Size Studies and the Thrill of Biological Discovery 207
Threats and Realities of Oil Pollution 217
Publications by Kees Vermeer 1963–1994 225
Acknowledgments 243
About the Author 245

Introduction

It is only in my late eighties, that I feel compelled to write about my experiences as an immigrant and ornithologist.

As a graduate student and a Canadian Wildlife Service (CWS) ornithologist, I enjoyed investigating different aspects of ornithology and publishing the research findings. As a recent immigrant, I felt useful by giving something tangible to Canadian society for providing me with new opportunities, which were unavailable to me in the Netherlands.

After retirement, I missed sharing biological discoveries with colleagues and students. I began writing short stories for family in the Netherlands. I had to learn how to write stories that would appeal to my family as most of my writing had been of a technical nature. I must have had some success with five of my fifteen nephews and nieces as they still correspond with me regarding these stories, which formed the beginning of my book, *Immigrant Gone to Heaven*. This is my first non-technical book, which also could be my last, as I am a few months shy of ninety. But come what may, the writing of this story has given me a new zest for life. It has given me the satisfaction of sharing it with others, who may enjoy reading and learning something from my life story.

The title of this book is from Rob Butler's tribute entitled *Kees Vermeer: Scientist and Conservationist*, in a joint conference program of the Colonial Waterbird Society and the Pacific Seabird Group in Victoria, British Columbia on November 8–12, 1995.

Rob's opening line is: *When Kees Vermeer set foot in British Columbia in April 1954, he must have thought he had died and gone to heaven.*

That line gave me the title for this book, *Immigrant Gone to Heaven*.

"Gone to heaven" means different things to different people. I found "heaven" when I began my MSc study on Glaucous-winged Gulls on Mandarte Island. It was not just the fieldwork I enjoyed, but much more so the pioneering research on the ecology of nesting gulls. I realized then that I had found my niche – conducting research, which I loved. I discovered that gulls have some similar behaviour to humans. They maintain a strong pair bond within and outside the breeding colony. Most gulls mate with the same partner year after year. Gulls maintain a strong family bonding. Both male and female share in the brooding of the eggs. The young stay with and are fed by the parents for several weeks after they leave the gull colony. As in human society, there are deviants. Just prior and at the time of egg laying, some nesting males frequently visit neighbouring females on their nest and attempt to rape them when their mates are absent. Most of the time the females resist violently by grabbing and pulling a wing of the advancing males.

Besides observing the behaviour of gulls on their nesting territories, I investigated other aspects of their biology. In one large chick addition experiment, I tested the clutch size hypothesis of David Lack, a distinguished ornithologist from Oxford University in England, who visited me on Mandarte Island. The result of my experiment did not support Lack's clutch size hypothesis and created a raging discussion on that subject. Ron Ydenberg, in his tribute in Part IV of this book, discusses this topic in detail.

The Mandarte Island study was just the beginning of my biological adventures and discoveries which led me to wild, unspoiled and beautiful places on Canada's frontiers where few or no people live.

PART I
Life as an Immigrant

From the Farm to a PhD

The story begins in 1953, with a seven-month training program in agriculture at an old sugar factory in Werkendam and on a farm in the adjacent Biesbosch in the Netherlands. Besides farmland, the Biesbosch is unique for having the largest freshwater and tidal wetlands within Europe. The name Biesbosch translates into forest of bulrushes.

Actual migration to Canada began on March 30, 1954, when I crossed the Atlantic by boat from Rotterdam to Halifax, after which I travelled across the continent by train to New Westminster in British Columbia. From there, a fieldman of the Christian Reformed Church drove me to the Fraser Valley, where I found work on two dairy farms, first at Deroche, and later at Chilliwack. My employment there lasted three months and spelled the end of my ten-month career as a farmer on both sides of the Atlantic. From then on my life took on a new direction, with different jobs and adventures until I realized I needed more education, and the sooner, the better.

In September 1956, I enrolled as a student at the University of British Columbia in Vancouver in a Bachelor of Science (BSc) program in geology and zoology. After obtaining my BSc degree in 1959, I took a year off from university to make a living and to consider the direction of further studies. After reaching a decision, I enrolled in a Master of Science (MSc) program in zoology at the University of British Columbia in 1960. I obtained an MSc degree in May 1963. In September of that year, I enrolled at the University of Alberta in Edmonton for a PhD study in zoology.

In the spring of 1966, I began writing my PhD thesis, at which time the director of the Canadian Wildlife Service (CWS) invited me to attend a movie at the university theater. Out of the blue, during intermission, he offered me the position of a biologist with CWS, which I accepted. My career with CWS began on July 1, 1966. In September 1967, I successfully defended my thesis and received a PhD degree in zoology. The following month I met Rebecca, an immigrant fresh from the Philippines and a graduate student at the University of Alberta. We got married at the Bureau of Vital Statistics in Edmonton on February 20, 1968.

Together, the CWS biologist position, a PhD degree, and my marriage to Rebecca constituted a natural ending to my life as a migrant. Therefore, I enclose "Wedding at Lunch Break" as the last relevant chapter of Part I – Life as an Immigrant.

Canada is a country of immigrants. There are many immigrant stories, and each one is different and tells something of how the Canadian fabric has evolved. When the years go by, these stories may become of historic interest and are worth preserving. My account is not a from rags to riches story, but that of an immigrant who tries to survive as best as he can while acquiring an education.

Biesbosch—My Last Station

Although I considered it earlier, I decided to prepare for emigration to Canada in earnest in March 1953. Since Canada needed farm workers, it seemed that the best way to prepare for emigration was to work on a farm. I met a teacher in Gorinchem who was enthusiastic about prospects in Canada and who had family on a farm in the Biesbosch. The teacher drove me to his relatives' farm by end of March 1953. When we arrived at the farm in the evening, a son of the Baelde family was plowing the fields on a tractor, with lights blazing. There was much to catch up on after the land had been inundated two months earlier during a disastrous storm and flood, called "the Ramp," when more than eighteen hundred people drowned and tens of thousands were forced to leave their homes.

The Baelde family greeted me enthusiastically and welcomed me to start work by milking cows at four o'clock the next morning. The Baelde family was thrifty and hardworking. My brother-in-law Adriaan Collee, who sold farm implements in the Biesbosch, told me later that if I could keep up with the Baeldes, I could survive anything! Since my visit was of an exploratory nature, and as I had not brought any proper work clothes, I asked if I could start work on April 1, to which they agreed. After my job started, I had no problem keeping up with the Baeldes. Not only that, I very much enjoyed the company of Henk and his brother, who were strong as oxen.

When my father died on April 25, 1953, I stayed home with my mother for the next five days. After I returned to the Biesbosch, Henk informed me that a training centre had just opened in an abandoned sugar factory at the edge of the Biesbosch, near a town called Werkendam, for prospective emigrants who wanted farm experience. I made inquiries at the training centre and the people in charge accepted me into their program. From May 4 on, I boarded at the factory and at six o'clock every morning, I rode my bicycle to Baeldes' farm. My workload was much lighter now, as I did not have to milk cows at four in the morning. I also worked five days instead of six days a week. My salary increased exponentially from fifteen guilders a month to thirty guilders a week, as the Dutch Government subsidized our wages by 50 percent. Best of all, the weekends were free, so I could stay with my mother, who after my father died, lived alone. I worked with the Baelde family for seven months and boarded at the sugar factory for six months.

Thirty prospective emigrants were enrolled at the training centre and boarded at the sugar factory. We slept upstairs in the factory on bunk beds, which was not always safe, as one night the fellow on the upper bunk crashed with boards and all on top of me. I was trapped with a board across my face and mouth preventing me from protesting until my bunkmate realized what had happened. Every day, we made our own breakfast, packed a lunch, and had dinner served downstairs by Moeke (mother) Bleijenberg at six o'clock, after our return from the farm. Some evenings we received practical instructions on farming techniques and equipment maintenance. We were brimming with enthusiasm and had great hopes for the future. That enthusiasm is reflected in Elseviers Weekblad article of October 31, 1953, entitled "Zij gaan om uit te zaaien en te maaien" (they go out to sow and mow).

Interesting are the comments in that article by H. A. van Luyk, Emigration Commissioner, who said: "We must do everything possible for our emigrants ...We plan to follow our countrymen in their foreign environment, and we will support and assist them when they encounter difficulties." Mr. van Luyk's expressed intentions were great and likely sincere, but I never felt that the Dutch Emigration Service followed my fate in Canada. Nevertheless, I was grateful to the Emigration Service for the help they provided in the Biesbosch, and for easing our path to Canada and other countries. That in itself makes me feel proud to be a Dutch Canadian.

Interesting also are the comments in that same article made by the remonstrant minister, Arend Jan Tellegen, a kind of *rara avis* among us emigrants, who said: "They talk too much in the Netherlands. We are too intellectual. Now I experience how wonderful it is to be in God's nature. Now I know what it means to be a farmer. To go out and sow and mow. I hope to do that soon in Alberta, in that great country of Canada, with its unlimited possibilities." I do not know if Arend Jan stayed with the program, as I no longer saw him at the factory three months before the program ended.

There are also the comments by seventeen-year old Jacque Sol, the youngest person among us. "I have no regrets," Jacque said. "The best thing is to go with the big tractors across the fields and plow the land. It is beautiful work that I soon hope to do in Canada. My friend Kooyman will go with me. Together we will do alright. We hope to leave in March 1954." I heard later from Jacque's friend Bert Kooyman that Jacque had problems, and died one or two years after he arrived in Alberta.

There is also the story of the thirty-two-year old Gerrit Verhagen, who continued his education over the years, but found that his life was not a bed of roses. "It is remarkable," Gerrit said, "that anything I started failed. It did not work. That is why I want to become a farmer. It really suits me best. I never knew that farming was such a beautiful vocation. I should have started earlier." Gerrit emigrated to Alberta. He never farmed, but rather became a draftsman with the Government of Alberta. I visited Gerrit many years later at his home in Edmonton, where he lived for the rest of his life. Gerrit died of a heart attack at the age of seventy-one while on a trip to California in 1992. Gerrit loved life and was a happy and cheerful person.

For more detailed comments and interviews with other emigrants, see Elsevier's article. Of the thirty prospective emigrants (not twenty-nine as stated by Elsevier), about one-fourth dropped out during the course of the program. Enclosed is a photo of twenty-five of us during peak attendance in front of the sugar factory. Five were absent at the time.

Most of my companions left the sugar factory by the last week of October. I began contract work for the last two weeks of that month loading and unloading sugar beets. Henk and his brother joined me, as many of the beets were from their farm. Other beets came from a neighbouring farm owned by a Mr. Kraker. Henk, who had become a true friend, suggested that I take on the beet job on contract, as he did not want me to be shortchanged by some farmers.

I earned a record wage of ninety guilders a week, which was much more than one would earn if working directly for a farmer. Sugar beets were loaded in the field and unloaded by a tractor and wagon at the harbour in Werkendam. The unloading of beets at the harbour was dangerous. We changed the upright position of one board of the wagon to horizontal, and anchored the board in place. We stood on the board, hanging over the ship. From there we moved the sugar beets into the empty ship below with shovels or forks as fast as we could. This was done from a great height, particularly at low tide, while standing on a slightly leaning board. One false or unlucky move would have finished us. Thinking about it still makes me shudder! But I was good at this contract job, and worked fast. So fast, that Henk told me his brother had a hard time keeping up with me. I just wanted to get off that board as quickly as possible.

I left the sugar factory by the end of October, but came back eight days later to join my friend, Kees Plasier, who was the only one still working on a farm called the Steenen Muur (stone wall). When I arrived at the factory that Sunday night, only Kees was there, in his bunk bed, upstairs. We both shivered at night in our bunk beds, because it was very cold and there was no heat in the building. The next morning, on November 9, 1953, we biked to the Steenen Muur, where the person in charge demonstrated how to milk cows with a milking machine (new at that time). After the demonstration, Kees and I cycled for one last time on roads surrounded by reeds waving in the wind, through the beautiful, fall-coloured Biesbosch. Kees wondered how things would be in Canada. I told him that everything would turn out alright. After that we parted ways; he cycled west to catch the train in Dordrecht, and I cycled east to catch the ferry at Sleeuwijk to Gorinchem.

I visited the factory in the Biesbosch in the summer of 1957. This was my first time back to the Netherlands from Canada since I left in 1954. I met Met Bleijenberg, and he told me that Moeke had passed away. The factory was strangely empty; there were no more emigrants. Met mentioned there were still migrants in 1954, but thereafter, there were few or none. It appears that attendance had been at its peak in 1953. I understand there was another training program for emigrants in the Northeast (Noordoost) polder, but not the numbers that had been enrolled at the Biesbosch in 1953. Perhaps there was no further need for the Dutch Government program to continue after the postwar migration wave started to wane.

Prospective emigrants to Canada and elsewhere.
Sugar Factory at Werkendam, Netherlands, summer 1953.
Front row: (L–R) Gerrit Ippel, de Boer (Mayor, Werkendam) van Lier (civil servant)
Second row: (L–R, squatting) Kees Schaay, Kees Vermeer (shawl), Jaap van Mill, Gerard van Swieten, Chris Dorsman, Gerrit Verhagen, Kees Schaap, Teun Smaal, Jacque Sol, Arduin
Third row: (L–R, standing) van Hoven (civil servant), Adri van Gulik, Arend Jan Tellegen (clergyman), Theo Sanders, Jo de Bruyne, Jelle Kok, Kees Plasier, Tom Riem, Chris Heybroek, Bert Kooyman, Filip Juch, Frits van Mechelen, Jenno van der Naald, Henk de Vries, Cor de Zeeuw, Martin Tijssen, Moeke Bleijenberg, Unknown behind Moeke, Met Bleijenberg

On the Move to Canada

On March 30, 1954, I left my home in Gorinchem for good. My brother Wim and sister Cato came by car to bring me to Rotterdam, from where I would sail to Canada. I said a quick farewell to my mother, leaving her with my sister-in-law Eggi to keep her company. My family and I thought it best that way, as she would be by herself after I left. Those of my family who lived close by promised to visit her regularly in the succeeding months.

In Rotterdam, I boarded the *Groote Beer* (Big Dipper), a converted troop transport ship. Eleven of my companions from the Biesbosch, where we had learned to farm in 1953, joined me. My closest friend from the Biesbosch was Kees Plasier. Some of my companions were married, others were single. When we sailed past Hoek van Holland into the North Sea, the sky looked grey and desolate. A handful of relatives waved from shore for one last time to those on board the *Groote Beer*. After dinner, I returned to my cabin and checked my handbag. I found a soft and half rotten banana tucked away among other items. My poor mother must have thought I would not get enough to eat the first day on the ship.

Groote Beer passengers list, March 30, 1954, Rotterdam to Halifax.

Immigrant Gone to Heaven

Mevr. L. Sytsma	De Heer M. Tyssen
De Heer T. Sytsma	Mevr. M. Tyssen
Mej. J. Sytsma	Jongeheer D. Tyssen
Mej. K. A. Sytsma	
De Heer L. Sytsma	De Heer C. van Uffelen
Jongejuffr. A. Sytsma	Mevr. C. van Uffelen
De Heer J. Szaraborak	
De Heer J. T. Teeuwen	De Heer J. C. van Veen
Mevr. J. T. Teeuwen	Mevr. J. C. van Veen
Jongejuffr. M. D. Teeuwen	Jongeheer J. A. van Veen
De Heer C. Terstall	Jongeheer E. J. van Veen
Mevr. C. Terstall	De Heer W. Veenbrink
De Heer C. Terstall	Mevr. W. Veenbrink
De Heer R. Terstall	De Heer J. C. Veenendaal
Jongejuffr. C. Terstall	De Heer B. G. Veens
De Heer J. Tigchelaar	Mevr. B. G. Veens
Mevr. J. Tigchelaar	De Heer P. W. Vercammen
De Heer F. M. Tiggeloven	Pater F. Verhagen
Mevr. F. M. Tiggeloven	De Heer G. Verhagen
De Heer J. Timmermans	De Heer C. Vermeer
De Heer M. Timmers	De Heer A. J. Vink
Mevr. M. Timmers	Mevr. A. J. Vink
Timmers	Jongejuffr. C. J. Vink
De Heer J. A. Tito	Jongeheer J. Vink
Mevr. J. A. Tito	Jongeheer J. Vink
Jongeheer J. A. Tito	Jongeheer G. Vink
Jongejuffr. J. M. Tito	De Heer G. Vink
De Heer J. P. Tolhuysen	Mevr. G. Vink
De Heer J. van der Toolen	Jongeheer B. Vink
Mevr. J. van der Toolen	Jongejuffr. W. A. Vink
Jongejuffr. E. J. van der	De Heer M. Visser
Toolen	Mevr. M. Visser
Jongejuffr. Y. M.	De Heer L. Ch. Vissers
Toolen	Mej. E. Vogel
De Heer J. J. den Tuinder	Mej. J. Vogel
Mevr. J. J. den Tuinder	De Heer J. Vogelzang
Jongejuffr. J. J. den Tuinder	Mevr. J. Vogelzang
Jongeheer J. J. den Tuinder	Jongeheer G. Vogelzang

Groote Beer **passengers list, page 13, De Heer C. Vermeer.**

Kees Vermeer

Menu

Ontbijt.
Grape Fruit
Havermout met Melk
—
Gekookt Ei
—
Boterhamworst
—
Edam Kaas-Aardbeien Jam
—
Wit-en Bruinbrood-Krentenbollen-Toast-Boter
—
Koffie-Thee
-:-

Middagmaal.
Potage St. Germain
—
Gebraden Varkenscarbonade
Gestoofde Bieten
Gekookte Aardappelen
—
Brood Boter
—
Icecream met Wafels
—
Vers Fruit
—
Koffie
-:-

Avondmaal.
Consommé Fermière
—
Gebraden Lamsbout
Wittekool in Saus
Gekookte Aardappelen
—
Brood Boter
—
Ananas Pudding
—
Vers Fruit
—
Koffie
-:-

Woensdag, 31 Maart 1954.

Groote Beer menu, March 31, 1954.

The next day, we arrived in the open Atlantic. After breakfast, I headed to the open deck. The sky was blue, but the winds had increased and the waves were larger. People began hanging over the railings and emptying their stomachs into the sea. I followed suit. Of my Biesbosch companions, only Kees seemed to be unaffected. Vomit was all over the deck; one had to walk very carefully not to slide into the large puddles of disgorged matter. Even though my stomach was upset, I still would visit the dining room, as I did not want my stomach to be empty most of the time. I spent as much time as possible on the open deck, where there was fresh sea air. The following days were not much better. The weather became rougher than before, and many of the seasoned crew became seasick, too. On some days, only a few passengers visited the dining room, which was roped off to prevent chairs and tables from sliding from one end of the room to the other and crashing. That went on with only few reprieves for at least a whole week at sea. I was glad to see the first land, which was Sable Island. I joined my companions to view the island. Although the waves were still rough, we laughed and joked, as we knew it would not be long before we reached Halifax, our port of disembarkation.

We arrived in Halifax harbour at about nine o'clock on the evening of April 7. The city was lit up and looked like a fairy-tale setting. A clergyman began a brief prayer, asking God to bless and guide the emigrants in their new country. We all felt happy as the ship finally came to rest, and we could shed the last remnants of our seasickness. We were happy that the rough ocean voyage was behind us.

The next morning, the emigrants (now immigrants) left the ship. It took only a few minutes to have our passports checked in the immigration hall, where our belongings were already stored. We crossed the railroad next to the hall, to the train station where we left our luggage. Kees and I explored nearby Halifax, where melting snow still covered the roadsides. My first impressions of Halifax were that the city was very colourful, because of the great variety of roof colours. However, the streets were dirty compared to those of a Dutch city, and the women were sloppily dressed compared to those in the Netherlands.

We entered a grocery shop where I bought a loaf of bread, peanut butter, some bananas, canned milk, and a can opener. The Dutch Government had provided me with thirty dollars to cover expenses for the train journey, and for the first days of our arrival at our final destination. That was plenty, as the exchange rate in 1954 was then close to four guilders per dollar. The amount of money met my needs and I thank the Dutch Government belatedly for that.

In the afternoon, we entered the train for our next journey. All immigrants had labels with numbers pinned to their jackets, coats, or dresses. It gave us the feeling of cattle being transported by rail. We removed the tags after one day. Train benches were made of wood, which could be extended for sleeping. At night, we were given blankets for cover. One Biesbosch companion, Martin Tijssen, and his wife and son, were not on board the train, and perhaps had left us in Halifax. That left eleven of us for the train journey. I became sick as I drank some of the canned evaporated milk, which I had mistaken for ordinary milk. Kees and I shared a train compartment. The train moved slowly and wound its way through Nova Scotia and New Brunswick. The steam locomotive would frequently sound its long warning call—wooo! ... wooo! .... wooo! Even months after my journey across Canada, I kept hearing that sound in my head!

Early the next morning, on April 9, Kees and I woke up to see steam and smoke rising from factories on the skyline of still-frozen Montreal. By noon we arrived in Toronto, where another Biesbosch friend, Kees Schaap, and his wife Gerry (now Grace), said farewell to us. In the Biesbosch, I often went fishing with Kees in the evening, as he was an ardent fisher. Kees Schaap was also an artist, and made many sketches. That came him into good stead in Canada. The Catharine Standard newspaper of St. Catharines, Ontario featured a story of Kees' accomplishments on March 3, 1977.

After the Toronto stop, ten of us continued our train journey across the bleak and wintery landscape of Ontario and Manitoba. Early in the morning of April 11, the train arrived in Winnipeg. When we opened the door and stepped onto the station platform, we were caught off guard by the brutally cold air, which greeted us in our thin Dutch jackets. Central Canada was much colder than we had expected at that time of year!

In Winnipeg, we had hot showers and lunch at the immigration centre near the train station. There I met another Biesbosch fellow; I had not seen him since 1953. His name was Kees Schaay. He and his wife Lenie, and their two sons, had come to Winnipeg earlier, and had stayed in the immigration centre. They had arrived in Halifax with the ship *Waterman* on April 2, 1954, six days before we disembarked from the *Groote Beer*. Early in the evening, Kees, Lenie, and I walked through Winnipeg and admired the city lights. We talked a lot, and were excited about our potential future in Canada. Soon after, Kees and Lenie found a job on a farm at Brandon, Manitoba.

When I returned late in the evening from the city to the train station, I learned that my friend Kees Plasier, together with three other Biesbosch companions—Cor de Zeeuw, Gerrit Verhagen, and Renso Zits—had left by train for Edmonton, Alberta. I did not see Kees Plasier again until twelve years later in Calgary, Alberta.

Late at night, I boarded the train for Calgary with the remaining five Biesbosch companions. Four of us, the brothers Tom and Peter Riem, Theo Sanders, and Gerard van Swieten, were married; Frits van Mechelen and I were bachelors. We arrived in Calgary early in the afternoon on April 12. A group of farmers, who knew of our arrival, entered the train to inspect us. They asked us to show our hands, which reminded me of the old slave trade. One farmer, impressed by the calluses still on my hands from working in the Biesbosch, wanted me to go with him immediately. I had a difficult time cooling his ardour, as I had different plans from what the immigration authorities had in mind for me.

In the Netherlands, I had received a piece of paper informing me that my destination in Canada would be Calgary. However, I already had my mind set on British Columbia (BC), because of its scenic beauty. After I learned I had to go to Calgary, I contacted Mr. Van de Velde, a fieldman of the Christian Reformed Church at New Westminster, BC, with whom I had corresponded. I asked him how I could change my point of destination. Van de Velde, an experienced fieldman, informed me that it would be difficult to make the authorities change their minds. He suggested that I buy a train ticket for New Westminster after I got off the train in Calgary.

After I shooed away the ardent farmer, I grabbed my old suitcase and army bag, and exited on the railroad side of the train station, while the others stepped out on the station platform. I had no time to say farewell to my Biesbosch companions under the circumstances. In the meantime, there was a roll call for the immigrants, who had arrived on the platform. Someone who had seen me getting out on the wrong side of the train, shouted: "Kees, they are calling your name!" I waved to him to keep quiet. I hastily turned the corner of the last train carriage, and there I caught the last glimpse of my Biesbosch companions standing on the platform. I did not see them again, except for Gerard van Swieten, whom I met forty-five years later in Victoria, BC. I was now the only Biesbosch person left to continue the journey farther west.

I hurried across the platform to the ticket office, where I planned to buy my ticket for New Westminster. Since my place of arrival was a Canadian National Railway (CN) train station, the ticket official informed me that I had to buy the ticket to New Westminster at the Canadian Pacific Railway (CP) train station somewhere else in Calgary. I took a taxi to the CP station and bought a ticket to New Westminster for about $6.50. There was plenty of time before the train arrived, and as I had not eaten for some time, I had my first meal in a nearby restaurant. I ordered a hamburger, an item I had not seen before. To me it looked like a flattened giant Dutch meatball. The hamburger was badly burnt. The reason I recall the incident so vividly is because I suffered terrible heartburn for several hours afterward.

After I boarded the train at six o'clock that evening, I took a seat on a hard wooden bench. I did not sleep much during the night that followed, and shifted my position constantly, leaning first on one arm and then the other. When I awoke the next morning, I saw the majestic, snowcapped Rocky Mountains, a sight I will never forget. After passing through the Rockies, I saw long stretches of beautiful large yellow flowers in ditches and marshes. I would have loved to examine the flowers from close up and smell them. Much later, I heard their name was Skunk Cabbage.

In the afternoon, the train passed through the Fraser Canyon, also with spectacular views and mountain slopes adorned with beautiful hues, reflecting different minerals. It was evening when we reached the Fraser Valley. There I saw children playing basketball in their backyards. It was a scene so familiar that it could have been anywhere in the Netherlands. It was getting dark when the train reached New Westminster. Although the scenery had been amazing, I felt tired and had a pounding headache on arrival after thirty-six hours with little or no sleep.

When I stepped off the train, I heard the familiar croaking of frogs, but the sound seemed to come from trees and not from ditches, as they did in Holland. It may have been the tree frog, Hyla regilla. Since I was a boy, I always had been interested in anything that crawled, crept, or croaked. After crossing one ocean by boat and one continent by train, I was happy to hear that familiar sound. My headache disappeared, and I began to relax. I felt home and among friends. Thank you, Hyla!

From the Farm to Alpine Meadows

When I arrived at the New Westminster train station on the evening of April 13, 1954, I asked a station officer if he could phone a certain Mr. Van de Velde, who was my contact person in that city. Mr. Van de Velde picked me up at the station and brought me to a small hotel, for which the rate was only one dollar per night. The bedroom was small, and contained the bare essentials; the toilets and bathrooms were located down the hall. A bath felt wonderful after a long and tiring journey.

Deroche

Mr. Van de Velde picked me up after breakfast the next morning. We drove to the Fraser Valley where we visited farmers and asked if they needed help. We were lucky on our third attempt. It was a dairy farm in a small village called Deroche. Of three Dutch farmhands at that farm, two of them had had a fight the day before. One of them left with a bloody nose after the fight, and I was the lucky person to fill his place.

I slept in a small shed in an orchard and boarded with Bill, the Canadian foreman. Seventy cows had to be milked, many of them by machine. I manually milked those that had problems with the milking machine. Bill and his wife, who was a teacher, were very hospitable. Bill encouraged me to read the local newspaper, and it was not long before I could understand and read English fluently. I also frequently took hot showers; it was pure joy after having been limited to only one bath a week in the Netherlands. In and near the orchard I watched nesting birds, which were new to me such, as Robins, Red-winged Blackbirds, and Kildeer Plovers. On the weekends, I would visit Mission, the nearest town, to have coffee with the other two farmhands. One of them, Walter, would drive us there in his small Austin. Walter would also drive us to see the Yale and Saddleback Tunnels in the Fraser Canyon beyond Hope.

One Sunday afternoon, I decided to visit my cousin Trijntje, who lived in Abbotsford. I phoned Trijntje, who was surprised to hear from me. After the phone call, I hitchhiked to Abbotsford, where I spent a very enjoyable hour with Trijntje and her husband, Klaas. After that, I hitchhiked back as it was becoming dark. I was lucky with my last ride; a kind gentleman drove a long distance out of his way to deliver me to the farm in Deroche. That visit had consequences, as two days later, I received a telephone call from a person called Nan from Chilliwack. Nan's wife, Marie, was the sister of Klaas in Abbotsford. Nan, who was the foreman on a farm near Chilliwack, told me his farmhand had left and that he urgently needed a replacement.

I had been on the farm for only one month in Deroche, and was reluctant to leave. I told Bill about the phone call, and he said it was for me to decide what to do but he would prefer me to stay. Since Bill would still have two farmhands if I left, I decided to join Nan, who picked me up the next day in Deroche and from there we drove to Chilliwack.

Chilliwack

For the next two months I worked with Nan, who was a good farmer, and loved his work. I learned new farming techniques from Nan; however, I did not get along with his boss, a vulgar person, and the owner of the farm. After the first month, I informed Nan he should look for a replacement, because I planned to leave the following month. Nan's attitude to me changed; he threatened that I could be deported back to the Netherlands. I did not take his threats seriously, and was still able to get along with him for the remaining month. I left the farm on July 14, on my birthday, for the town of Chilliwack. That was the end of my farming career in Canada. I did not regret that, as I had been paid only eighty dollars per month, with room and board. At that rate, it would be a long time before I could afford to own a farm.

In Chilliwack, I took up room and board with the Niessen family, and became friends with their son Arie. I contacted the local employment office, and the next day I got a job as a sign painter's assistant. The job lasted for three weeks and paid one dollar per hour. Most of my job consisted of painting the frames of huge advertising boards along the highway. To paint the upper part of the frame, I had to stand on a wooden board, which served as scaffold. One time the board broke, but I was still able to grab the upper frame and hold on while leaning against the fresh green paint, high above the ground. My foreman became very nervous, but I assured him I could hang on for a while, and that he should calm down and get a ladder, which he did after some confusion. My pants had dropped off in the meantime, and my bare white belly and shorts had turned dark green. When I descended in my green outfit, my foreman looked stunned at my appearance. Relieved, he began to laugh hilariously.

Manning Park

The sign painting job finished in early August, so I visited the employment office for the next job. The next day, I was hired by American Metals, a mining company, to work as a geologist's assistant at a mining camp in Manning Provincial Park in the beautiful and rugged Cascade Mountains. The base camp of American Metals was situated along the Trans-Canada Highway between Hope and Princeton. That proved to be the best and most enjoyable job during my first year in Canada. Not only that, the company paid me $225 per month with room and board, which was three times more than what I had earned on the farm. I assisted a geologist nicknamed Rocky, a visiting geologist from Egypt. We got along well. The work consisted of measuring with a Brunton compass the strike and dip of rock outcrops, and examining them with a pocket lens for mineral content. I enjoyed the work and became interested in geology, so much so that when I went to university two years later, I took several geology courses in my undergraduate years and majored in the subject.

The fieldwork was conducted from a few cabins at the edge of the tree line. At that altitude, there were still patches of snow in August. The snow higher up on the alpine meadows was rapidly melting, after which beautiful yellow glacier lilies, red moss campions, blue lupins, purple penstemon, western anemones with white woolly heads, and sweet-scented mountain valerians carpeted the mountain slopes.

I liked the area around the cabins where bold and inquisitive Gray Jays (Whisky Jacks) came for food, which we held out for them. I stayed there by myself during the weekends while Rocky and the others drove down the narrow mountain trails by jeep to the main base camp along the Trans-Canada Highway. When they returned the following Monday, they brought provisions and extra apple pies, which the cook at the base camp had made especially for me, as he knew that nobody loved his apple pies as much as I did.

I hiked over mountaintops and slopes and enjoyed listening to the hoarse calls of Ravens, and was excited to encounter my first black bears. I discovered an old molybdenum and silver mine, which had been operated by Finnish miners in the early 1910s and 1920s. The Finns used donkeys and cables to transport the ore. Dried-out donkey dung was still present in the old stables. I stayed overnight in one of their old and well-built cabins, and cut a block of ice with an axe in a nearby mountain creek to melt in a pan over fire in a woodstove for my morning tea, while a few wood rats in the cabin curiously stared at me. When heavy snow returned in late September, we could not continue our fieldwork. I was sorry to leave the beautiful alpine meadows. After one night at the base camp, I returned to Chilliwack on October 2, 1954.

**Lupins (blue) and wooly heads of Western Anemone (white)
at Manning Park
(Photo Credit: Annetta J. Photography).
Most people never see the anemone flowers because the plant
pops up immediately after the snow has melted.**

My Salvation Army Home

When I emigrated from the Netherlands to Canada in April 1954, I had no inkling where my next home would be, except that it would be somewhere in British Columbia. Six months after my arrival in BC, and after various short term jobs, I ended up living briefly with my cousin Walter's family on Lulu Island, while working as a sign painter in downtown Vancouver. One evening, while removing red feather signs off windows, as it was the end of the Red Feather Campaign, I happened to scrape signs off the Salvation Army House on 500 Dunsmuir Street. I asked a friendly woman at the reception desk if there were any room vacancies. Her name was Ruth, and she asked me where I hailed from. When I answered Holland, to my surprise, Ruth addressed me in Dutch, and informed me she had been a Salvation Army officer in the Dutch East Indies (Indonesia), where she learned the Dutch language. Ruth told me there were several vacant rooms. The rent was six dollars per week with weekly cleaning and fresh bed linens and towels. It was a fantastic bargain, even for 1954!

A few days after my inquiry, I was laid off from my sign painting job. I told Walter that it would be more convenient for me to move to downtown Vancouver to look for work. On November 7, Walter helped me move to my new residence on 500 Dunsmuir Street. I explored my surroundings to determine where to shop and eat and where I could find a job. I also attended a Remembrance Day service at nearby Victory Square on November 11, and was impressed with the military drill by the Royal Canadian Mounted Police. It was my first Remembrance Day experience. Soon after, I mingled with war veterans who gathered in the Dunsmuir House lobby for social activities. The veterans related stories of Vimy

Ridge and other WWI battles. In exchange, I told them about my WWII experience in the Netherlands.

Most lodgers at the Dunsmuir House were Canadians, but there were also other nationalities including a few Dutch. One was Mike Schipper, who became my best friend in Vancouver. Mike, who hailed from Zaandam, where his father owned a cheese factory, had a steady job as a nurse at the Vancouver General Hospital. On the weekends, Mike and I roamed the streets and waterfront of downtown Vancouver. Mike, who tried to keep to a diet, alternated between fasting and binging on food. He could not resist apple pie à la mode, to which I treated him on several occasions. He was also a smoker, and had tried to quit many times. Once he was so disgusted with his smoking habit, he threw his pack of cigarettes onto a nearby roof. A few days later, the urge to smoke became so strong, that he almost fell out of the window trying to rake in that pack of cigarettes he had thrown away. We had a great laugh about that.

Another lodger I became acquainted with was Roy Walker, a WWII veteran. Roy had served in the Netherlands, and fondly related his experience there to Mike and me. Roy occasionally treated us to a three-course dinner in a restaurant for sixty-five cents each. Roy had enrolled as a student at the University of British Columbia (UBC), where he completed his study for a master's degree in sociology. Roy had taken courses in psychology, which made him prone to giving me advice to use psychology in tackling a problem. Both Mike and Roy became my friends for life. Mike returned to the Netherlands several years after I had left Dunsmuir House, and Roy went to live with his sister in California a few years after he obtained his master's degree. I kept in contact with Roy and Mike until they died in 1999 and 2005 respectively.

On December 5, 1954, I had a surprise delivery of two large suitcases from Holland filled with goodies such as chocolate letters, almond pastries, marzipan, Dutch speculaas cookies, syrup waffles, and other items such as scarves, gloves, and Dutch magazines. My mother and sister Cato had prepared the suitcases for my first St. Nicholas' Day in Canada. I invited Mike, Roy, and some other fellows to my room that day where we had a great time sharing the delicacies while Mike and I fondly reflected on past St. Nicholas' Eve celebrations on December 5 in the Netherlands. The timing of the delivery of the suitcases by ship across the Atlantic and by rail across Canada was incredible!

My job hunting in winter was not as successful as it had been in summer. However, I did not mind, as I had more free time and had saved enough money to last through the winter. One of my first jobs was to store cowhides in a warehouse; I was the only Dutchman among a group of Italians and Ukrainians. It was the most disgusting work I ever had. We carried stinking cowhides, some with maggots, beneath a roof with a ceiling so low, we had to walk with bended backs for hours. When the day's work was done, I rode a bus home in my terribly smelly clothes, as there was no place to change at the warehouse. I had all the room I wanted in the bus as people avoided me. I was happy when the employer suddenly terminated everyone's job. The next job was in construction, which lasted three weeks. The foreman fired me because I did not want to join the trade union. The membership fee was ninety dollars, which I did not want to pay, not knowing how long the job would last. Moreover, much of the work had to be done under miserable conditions. I had to work in tight trenches filled with water, as it rained most of the time.

In January and February of 1955, I hardly worked at all. I had a few odd jobs, one which I will never forget. It was a longshoreman's job of shovelling grain in the hold of a ship in Vancouver harbour. I and a few others wore face masks, which did little to prevent fine dust from settling in our eyes and noses. The ship's hold filled up quickly with grain, and only one small opening remained open for exit. When that exit became covered with grain, there was total darkness. We had to dig furiously to escape. It took days for the fine black dust to clear from my nose. For most of March, I dug ditches for sewer pipes. Looking back, I surely went through many jobs during my first year in Canada. I have no regrets; it was an interesting learning experience. I was willing to try any job, even unpleasant ones, to make ends meet and to explore the opportunities which came along.

Living among immigrants of different nationalities, students, war veterans, and transients from other Canadian cities and provinces in Dunsmuir House, as well as being exposed to begging alcoholics and vagrants in adjacent downtown streets, turned my thoughts to what I wanted to achieve and what I desired to avoid. In the beginning of April, I made up my mind to improve my education and therefore my chances for permanent work. I made inquiries at normal school, an institute for training teachers. I was advised that I could enroll in September. From September 1955 to May 1956, I attended normal school. I decided not to pursue a teaching career, but used the gained knowledge as a stepping stone for enrolling in a Bachelor of Science program at UBC in September 1956.

I left Dunsmuir House in January 1957 to be closer to UBC, but I never will forget my first Canadian home on Dunsmuir Street. To this day, I am thankful to the Salvation Army for giving me a home when I needed one. The Salvation Army has remained my favourite charity because of my early immigrant experience. As part of a Sidney Rotary program, my wife and I ring kettle bells for the Salvation Army in front of the Sidney Liquor Store each Christmas season.

Salvation Army's Dunsmuir House
(Photo Credit: Rick Horne for Vancouver Heritage Foundation).
Dunsmuir House was once a prestigious hotel built in 1908 (according to some sources, in 1913). In 1947, it became a shelter for war veterans. The Salvation Army took over the building in 1949 and made it into a shelter and social services centre called Dunsmuir House. I lived in Dunsmuir House from November 1954 to January 1957, except for the

summers of 1955 and 1956, when I held jobs in the BC interior. Certain buildings are anchors for people living at the edges of the city's economy. Dunsmuir House is such a building. It sheltered immigrants, students, and war veterans over the years until they gained strength and opportunities to play active and constructive roles in the Canadian fabric. The Citizens' Rehabilitation Council of Greater Vancouver, the Salvation Army and the Vancouver Heritage Foundation all helped to save Dunsmuir House for those who needed a refuge and a home. As such, Dunsmuir House has become a lasting beacon for those in need whatever, their origin and destiny.

Living in a Boxcar

In April 1955, the Vancouver Employment Office notified me about the availability of a summer job for a technician to survey land along the railroad between Terrace and Kitimat in northern British Columbia. The surveyor in charge was a Mr. Christie, who was semi-retired and about seventy years of age. My job was to assist a young surveyor, called Bryan Berting.

At the end April, four of us—Mr. Christie, Bryan, Miles (an old survey hand and friend of Christie), and I—left Vancouver by car for Terrace. We stayed overnight first in Williams Lake, and then in Prince George, where provisions were bought for the fieldwork. After a night in Prince George, we left early the next morning for Terrace. The road between Prince George and Terrace at that time was gravel. Our first stop was at Vanderhoof, a small village where we visited a small grocery store. A group of kids greeted us; to them we were a big event. After the rest stop we continued our journey, it was cold, and ice still covered Fraser Lake along the highway. We made another rest stop in Smithers, which was also in the grip of winter. When we reached Hazelton, trees were sprouting leaves, indicating we were entering the Pacific coastal zone. We arrived in Terrace late at night.

Snow still covered the mountains around Terrace, a small town on the Skeena River. The first week we stayed in a motel, after that we slept in boxcars stationed on a railroad track. A sixty-year-old woman joined our boxcar camp; she would be our cook for the summer. In Terrace, we began our first surveys. After that, our camp moved to a site between Terrace and Kitimat, close to a lake called Lakelse Lake. Our camp was at one side of the main railroad track, and Lakelse Lake at the other. More people joined our team; one of them was a French Canadian called Albert. Albert was an interesting character who lived in a small cabin with a large garden in Terrace, where he spent his summers. In winter, Albert operated a trapline in the mountains, where he trapped animals for their fur. Another employee was Roy, a Finnish Canadian and a lumberjack by profession. By August, our team further increased with the arrival of a Ukrainian Canadian, called Harry. Our survey team had an international flavour. We all got along well, but had reservations regarding Mr. Christie, who we called Black Peter, after the Dutch Santa Claus helper. Bryan became a close friend. Roy wanted to start a homestead with me, but I had plans to further my education after the survey work was done.

Initially, I was an axeman, who had to cut and clear trees along transects in order for Bryan to take precise measurements with a transit instrument mounted on a tripod. Later, I doubled as a chainman, measuring with a metal chain the distance travelled along a transect. The others operated either as axemen or chainmen, except Harry, who was hired to operate a motorized speeder on the railroad track. The speeder was brought in by August.

Albert entertained us with many stories of his encounters with black bears, grizzly bears, and wolverines along his traplines in winter. We had several encounters with black bears ourselves, and once with a wolf. The wolf suddenly appeared out of nowhere, close to us on the railroad track. I was not aware of its presence until Bryan asked me to look through the transit scope. I was stunned, as the wolf looked so big through the scope. It looked like I could touch the animal. That particular wolf was not afraid of us and seemed to challenge our presence. Sometimes it was lying down on a mossy spot near the railroad track and examining us with its very cool eyes, which made us feel uneasy about its intentions. It was the only time I saw a timber wolf that was not afraid of humans. Most of the time, wolves seemed to avoid us and we rarely got glimpses of them at a distance.

I also enjoyed observing the smaller forest creatures such as red squirrels, chipmunks, and skunks. Skunks were very common around our camp and were not afraid of us. If we came too close for comfort, they just lifted their tails to make their intentions known. We initially thought it funny and ignored their intentions, until somebody was sprayed. After that, we retreated immediately. We also saw Ruffed and Spruce Grouse. We could approach courting male Spruce Grouse within a few feet.

For entertainment, we visited the town of Kitimat to which we hitchhiked by train. The train, which passed by twice a day from Terrace, brought our mail, which was thrown off the train at our campsite. If we gestured that we needed a ride, the engineer would stop the train and let us climb aboard. Life was simple in the bush!

Once in Kitimat, we visited the beer parlor to have a few drinks. We were careful not to become involved in fights, which frequently occurred in or near the parlor. Most fights were over women, which were scarce in Kitimat. The vast majority of inhabitants were men. There were thousands of them compared to a few dozen women! About 90 percent of the men were Portuguese who worked for the Alcan aluminum plant. Portuguese was therefore the main language spoken in town.

In August, we often travelled by speeder along the railroad track, as survey sites were now farther from our camp. We had to be careful not to use the speeder at times when the train would pass by. If one had come by unexpectedly, we would have to move the heavy speeder quickly to the side of the track. Fortunately, we never had to. With our speeder, we enjoyed riding over an extraordinarily built wooden trestle spanning a canyon near our campsite. It was an exciting and unusual way of travelling through forests and marshlands.

At the end of August, I cut my shin with an axe, and had the cut stitched by a doctor in Terrace. The cut was minor, but from Bryan I heard that Mr. Christie thought the cut would affect my performance and planned to fire me. After it became apparent that such was not the case, Mr. Christie changed his mind. From that experience, I learned that we could be dismissed for the slightest reason. When I later informed Mr. Christie that in September I planned to attend normal school in Vancouver, he told me that the survey work was of national importance, and I should forget about going to school. I took notice of what he said, and planned accordingly.

When I received my paycheque at the end of August, I packed my old army bag and said farewell to my coworkers in the evening. They all wished me well and completely supported my plans. I also contacted a floatplane operator in Kitimat and asked when his plane would depart the next morning. The plane would leave Kitimat harbor at 7:30. I estimated the time it would take to walk with a fully packed army bag from the campsite along the railroad track to Kitimat harbour. I set my alarm clock for one o'clock. After the alarm rang, I quickly dressed and hustled out of the boxcar. I waited until my eyes got used to the darkness, and began walking along the track with the army bag slung over my shoulder. It was an exciting journey, with wolves howling in a swamp at one side of the track, while patches of phosphorescent tree bark gleamed eerily green on the other side. Every half hour I rested briefly. When it became light, I quickened my step. It was near seven o'clock when I arrived at the Kitimat railroad station. I still had to cross town to the harbour, which took another half hour. I reached the floatplane with only a few minutes to spare! We flew first to Prince Rupert, and from there by another plane to Vancouver.

I heard later from Bryan that when I did not show up for breakfast the next morning, Mr. Christie asked where Gus was. Gus was my name at the camp. According Bryan, when he told him that Gus (Kees) had left for Vancouver, Mr. Christie looked utterly shocked.

Before the day's work.
(L–R) Albert, Bryan, Roy, Gus (Kees), and Miles

Survey crew on a motorized speeder.
(L–R) Mr. Christie, Roy, Albert, Miles, Bryan, Harry, and Kees

Survey crew on a manually operated speeder.
(L–R) Kees, Roy, Miles (behind Roy), Albert, Mr. Christie, and Bryan

Kees and Roy resting on a manual speeder.

Kees and Roy crossing a trestle. Rectangular frame on left is a speeder parking space in case of emergencies.

Student Life and Journey to Holland

During the winter of 1955–56, I attended normal school in Vancouver. I enjoyed the coursework, but less so the two months of teaching in rough districts of downtown Vancouver, which was part of the curriculum. The latter seemed to be more about keeping discipline than teaching. Moreover, the coursework whetted my appetite for further studies of the natural sciences. After running transect lines for a pipeline project in the Okanagan during the summer, I enrolled at the University of British Columbia (UBC) in Vancouver in September 1956. I could begin in the second year of university, as I received credit for attending normal school. I still resided at the Salvation Army at Dunsmuir House in downtown Vancouver, from where I travelled by bus to UBC.

Student Life

I enjoyed my courses in natural science such as biology, zoology, and geology. I also took anthropology and advanced German; the latter was a foreign language requirement for a Bachelor of Science program. At that time, one had a choice of French, German, or Russian. I chose German, because it was the easiest foreign language for me. I took anthropology, because the behaviour and physical and social relationships of past and present cultures of humankind fascinated me. I had read several books by Margaret Mead, who was a renowned anthropologist.

At the university, I met three Dutch students: Jack Boulogne, Rob Luning, and Ben Wisseling, who became my friends. Jack was enrolled in philosophy and physics, Rob in geology, and Ben in forestry. We often met at International House, a wooden hut on campus, which was a meeting place for students of all nationalities. It was also a great place to have coffee or lunch between classes.

After Christmas, Rob and I visited the campus to check our marks that were posted in different buildings. With apprehension, we searched lists with names and marks, as it was our first semester and the marks were important for assessing our capabilities. Many other students did the same. I was happy to receive a B average in all subjects in my first attempt at university. That took the burden off my shoulders. We treated ourselves to a large plate of chop suey in a Chinese restaurant off campus. Now we really could enjoy the remainder of our holiday!

After New Year's, Jack and I looked for a place near campus where we could rent rooms, as it would save travel time between downtown Vancouver and UBC. We found a place on Ninth Avenue, about three blocks from campus. Our landlady was Mrs. Florence Bradshaw, a seventy-five-year old woman. Jack and I liked Florence. She was a feisty woman of Scottish descent who loved watching boxing on television. She would hold a cigarette in one hand and a glass of Irish whisky in the other while shouting "Beat the hell out of him, Charlie!"

As Florence tried to save on heating costs, there was a constant battle over the thermostat setting. The thermostat was at the entrance of the stairway. Before we went upstairs to our rooms to study, we switched the thermostat setting to keep our rooms sufficiently warm.

Before Florence would go to sleep in her bedroom downstairs, she would shout from the bottom of the stairs, "Are you warm enough up there, boys?" to which we replied "Yes, Florence." She then would lower the thermostat. After we thought she was asleep, we sneaked downstairs and turned the thermostat up again. The thermostat game went on for that whole semester, and not a bad word was said.

When I wrote to my mother about our landlady loving whisky and wearing scanty nighties, she warned me to watch out for "Potiphar's wife." My family in Holland had quite a laugh when I wrote back, "Do not worry, Mother, Potiphar's wife is seventy-five years old!" With all her eccentricities, Florence was a good-hearted woman. She sometimes cooked for us, which was much appreciated, as we did not have much time to prepare our meals. On the weekends, the four of us—Ben, Rob, Jack and I—treated ourselves to Chinese food in a nearby restaurant. We loved those occasions; they were a highlight in our frugal student life.

At the end of April, our final exams started. Many weeks before the exams, we reviewed what we had studied, trying to cram as much information into our heads as possible. Those were not fun days, as there was so much to read, digest, and memorize. Except for meals, we hardly had time for anything else. I felt relieved after the last exam. Now I had time to prepare for my first return to Holland.

Bus Journey from Vancouver to New York

I looked forward to visiting Holland and seeing my mother and the rest of the family. I discussed my plans with an agent to travel by Greyhound bus across the continent to New York, from where I would sail to Rotterdam. The bus itinerary was as follows: from Vancouver, Canada, to Seattle, then Portland, Salt Lake City, Denver, Kansas City, Chicago, Grand Rapids, and Detroit in the United States, and from there to Hamilton, Canada, where I planned to visit my cousin Sije and his wife, Sjaan. I had not been to the United States before, and wanted to see some of the big American cities. In Grand Rapids, I planned to visit my friend George, who was enrolled in a teacher training program at Calvin College. From Hamilton, I would continue my journey via Buffalo and Albany to New York.

My bus journey was sometimes tiring, but always interesting. I met all kinds of people; I took a picture of the Mormon Tabernacle at Salt Lake City; I had a long discussion with a Mormon on the bus who wanted to convert me; I visited a wild bird aviary in Kansas City; I had my clothes stolen when I took a quick shower in a Chicago bus depot; I visited George and stayed overnight at Calvin College; I was impressed by the solid and sombre look of the brick buildings at Grand Rapids; and I finally arrived at Sije and Sjaan's residence.

My arrival at Sije and Sjaan's place was hilarious. I took a taxi from the bus station and arrived at midnight. The door was locked and everybody was asleep. I picked up some small stones and threw them at an upstairs window. Sije opened the window and sleepily asked "Who are you?" I replied, "I am Kees Vermeer and I have just arrived." Sije shouted, "I do not believe you!" and closed the window. I picked up some more stones and threw them against the window. When Sije opened the window again, he shouted "What do you want?" I asked him to open the door, and when he did, we embraced and had a big laugh. Sjaan joined us and we talked all night until late in the morning. We had so much to share after not having seen each other for ten years.

Of all my cousins, Sije was closest to me. As a boy, I spent my school vacations with Sije and Sjaan when they lived among the tulip fields near Keukenhof. I would see them again twenty-five years later, when they arrived unannounced—as I did in Hamilton—at our door in Sidney, British Columbia. They enjoyed their visit so much that they spent their holidays with us for the next five years.

After two days with Sije and Sjaan, I continued my bus journey to New York. It was around four o'clock the next morning when I arrived there. I stretched out on a bench at the bus depot and went to sleep. I woke up with a bang and a sharp pain in my belly. A black policeman had struck me with a rubber baton and told me it was forbidden to sleep on benches. He could have used a civilized way to tell me! I thought it was a racist act. I took a taxi to the local YMCA, rented a room, and slept for the rest of the morning. In the afternoon, I visited the Empire State Building and enjoyed beautiful views of New York from there. The next morning, I left New York for Rotterdam aboard a Holland America Liner.

Arrival in Holland

The sea voyage went quickly. The sea was calm and the sailing smooth. I arrived in Rotterdam on May 26, 1957, and boarded the train to Gorinchem, where my mother lived. The door of my mother's house was locked. I was not surprised, as I had not informed her of the exact day of my arrival. An upstairs window at the front of the house was slightly open. I climbed up to the window, entered the bedroom, and opened the front door. Little in the house appeared to have changed since I left in 1954. In the evening, I walked the familiar streets and noted that people left their curtains wide open while glued to their television. It was as if they were showing off their new acquisitions. When I left Holland in 1954, there were no televisions in living rooms and curtains were drawn at night. The television age had changed all that, bringing the outside world directly into the Dutch living rooms.

When my mother arrived the next day, she was surprised to see me. We spent a leisurely three weeks together, and I often cycled through the Dutch polder. After that, I felt I had seen enough of the "old country," and was eager to return to Canada.

Return to British Columbia and Summer Employment

I sailed from Rotterdam to New York on June 18, 1957, and from there took the Greyhound bus to Vancouver. I was back in what I felt was my real home after an exciting journey, mixing a little bit of my past life in Holland with the present in Canada.

After arriving in Vancouver, I stayed with Florence Bradshaw, and within a few days found a summer job as a surveyor's assistant at a logging camp at Port McNeill on northern Vancouver Island. The job, which lasted two months, helped finance my next year of university. In early September, at a student party, the host asked each of us what we had done during the past summer. After I told him how I had spent my summer, he said, "Kees, you accomplished more than any of us; you made the journey to Holland and still earned enough during the summer to continue your university studies!" My host's compliment made me feel proud of what I had accomplished.

**Visit with my cousin Sije and family in Hamilton, Ontario, 1957.
Kees with Sije's family.**

**Leaving Rotterdam for New York, 1957.
Mother, sister Cato, and Kees on board a Holland America Liner
at Rotterdam.**

Finding my Niche

In 1959, I finished my Bachelor of Science (BSc) program at the University of British Columbia. I had taken two options for my BSc program—zoology and geology—because I had an interest in paleontology, which needed knowledge of both subjects. Dr. Louis Leakey's discoveries of hominids in the Rift Valley of Africa and the process of human evolution fascinated me.

I also had become a Canadian citizen in July 1959, five years after I entered Canada as an immigrant. I still recall the citizenship ceremony for the forty new citizens, which was presided over by a judge. He interviewed each prospective citizen with questions relating to the Canadian Parliament, history, and geography. When he came to me as the last person to welcome, he looked at my occupation and asked, surprised, "You are a student at UBC?" When I told him I had just finished my BSc, he became excited and forgot to test my knowledge of Canada. Instead, he talked enthusiastically about his daughter, who had enrolled in her first year of university.

Since I did not have sufficient funds to attend university in the fall of 1959, I decided to take a year off. Taking out a student loan as other students did was not my way, and would have only be a last resort. As I had a year to work and save enough to support further studies in September 1960, I decided to explore the southern United States and Mexico from the end of November 1959 to early January 1960.

California

I left Vancouver by Greyhound bus for California. I had a suitcase and an army bag, which were stored beneath the bus. The army bag contained an umbrella tent and a sleeping bag in case I wanted to camp along the way. The first place I camped was near San Clemente, California. I took a taxi to a state park along the beach, where I pitched my tent. I relaxed there for a week and did some bird-watching, reading, swimming, and with fascination, watched Monarch butterflies swarming in huge numbers over a grove of trees.

Mexico

After one week at San Clemente, I moved on to Nogales on the US-Mexican border, where I waited a long time for a bus, which went to Mexico City. Entering a Mexican border town gave me a perspective on life in a developing country. Life there looked very dismal compared to that in Canada. Prostitution seemed to be a main source of income; I could hardly walk a block without being propositioned.

Late in the afternoon, I left Nogales by "chicken bus," in other words, a bus overloaded with passengers, chickens, and other livestock. After a few hours, the bus broke down and we all had to get out. After waiting outside in the dark for a mechanic, who did some repairs, we continued our journey. Toilet facilities were filthy at rest stops. At one stop, I swung from a rope over an open pit doing my "business" in full view of other passengers while vultures waited on a nearby fence for crumbs. Kids sold tamales and other foods for a few pesos at rest stops. Once I bought a tamale and took a bite, but spat it out at once, as both the tamale and shrimp inside were not cooked.

When I arrived in Mexico City, I rented a hotel room for two nights; the service was good and the bed clean. Traffic in the city was fierce; and nobody seemed to stop for pedestrians. Construction was going on near my hotel; I felt sorry for the labourers who walked on bare feet and in torn clothing over narrow boards, carrying huge baskets on their heads loaded with sand, gravel, and cement. Regardless of their conditions, the Mexicans seemed to take it in stride and make the best of it. After a few days in the city, I decided to leave Mexico, and boarded a bus for Texas.

Texas

I got off the bus in Houston, and rented a housekeeping room for the next few weeks. I was surprised to see that restaurants segregated white and coloured persons. When I took a seat at the counter in a downstairs restaurant for coloured persons in a department store, the white server became very upset, and told me the restaurant for whites was upstairs. On one occasion, I took a local bus, with whites sitting in the front and blacks in the back. To test the colour barrier, I took a rear seat. The bus driver shouted that I had to come to the front of the bus. When I did not obey his command immediately, he slammed on the brakes and stopped the bus in the middle of traffic. He was furious, and told me to get off the bus if I would not take a front seat immediately. He wondered where I came from that I would do such a thing. My test proved that the colour barrier was for real!

On some days, I visited the public library to read newspapers and magazines such as *National Geographic* and *Scientific American*. I also visited the employment office and received a social security card and number, even though I did not ask for it. The man who gave me the card was very friendly. He asked about my work experience, and I told him I was a student with knowledge of geology. He gave me the address of a mining company, which I visited soon after. A geologist tested my knowledge by throwing from across the table rocks containing different minerals and asked me to identify them. He was so surprised that I could identify all of them correctly that he hired me on the spot. He informed me that I would need to take three months training in Houston, after which I would be sent to an isolated spot in the Libyan desert. The starting salary would be twelve thousand dollars per year plus all expenses, including board and travel between Libya and the United States. That was good money at that time, with which one could have bought an operating business or farm in a few years. It was tempting. After thinking it over for a day, I decided to turn the job down. I was not ready to live in a trailer in the Libyan desert.

After Christmas, I took a bus to Abilene to visit Cor, an old friend with whom I served in the Dutch Army. Cor attended a theological college and planned to become a minister at the church associated with that college in the Netherlands. I spent New Year's with Cor and his wife Jetske, and reminisced about events we shared in the Netherlands. A few years later, they returned to the Netherlands, but to Cor's great disappointment, he was never ordained as a minister, although he led the congregation there for the rest of his life. Although Cor died nearly thirty years ago, Jetske still goes to that American church, whose members she considers her family.

Alabama

After New Years's, I moved on to Mobile, Alabama, where I rented a cabin for a week in a state park along the Gulf of Mexico. Armadillos roamed around my cabin; I picked one by its tail and admired its armoured outfit. I relaxed at the park, and by the second week in January, I packed up my belongings and returned by bus to Vancouver, as it was time for me to earn an income and begin saving for university studies.

Back in British Columbia

My first job was as a surveyor's assistant in a logging camp at Port Moresby in the Queen Charlotte Islands (Haida Gwaii) where it rained every day for the whole of February. After one month, I developed acute tonsillitis, because I was allergic to smoke and had to share my sleeping quarters with a logger who smoked constantly. The logger wanted the bedroom window closed at all times, thereby containing his smoke within the room. As there was no alternative sleeping accommodation, I quit the job and flew back to Vancouver. There I received penicillin injections, which helped me to recover from tonsillitis.

From the beginning of April to early August 1960, I worked at the Biological Station at Departure Bay, Nanaimo. I assisted Dr. Kees Groot, who conducted experiments with salmon smolts to determine if these smolts used the position of the sun and celestial constellations for their migration from spawning areas to the ocean. Some of those studies were conducted at Babine Lake and Babine River in northern British Columbia. The studies were very interesting, and because of that experience, I made up my mind to study living things rather than going into the field of paleontology. I just had not made up my mind which living things. When Kees took me in a small boat into Departure Bay one day, I made up my mind.

Kees, who was also an avid nature photographer, took pictures of nesting Glaucous-winged Gulls on Snake Island, a small island in that bay. As I always had an interest in birds, I became intrigued with the behaviour of the nesting gulls.

To explore possibilities of conducting a study on Glaucous-winged Gulls, I contacted Rudi Drent, a graduate student I knew from UBC. At that time, Rudi studied the nesting biology of Pigeon Guillemots on Mandarte Island, a small Island near Sidney on Vancouver Island. Rudi invited me to Mandarte Island, and during a long weekend in May, I visited him there. I discussed my plans to study Glaucous-winged Gulls on Mandarte Island, where there was a large gull colony. Rudi supported my plans enthusiastically and recommended me to his supervisor, Dr. Miklos Udvardy, to conduct my studies under his supervision. Dr. Udvardy accepted me, and that was the beginning of my career as a seabird biologist!

Salmon smolt observation tank at Babine Lake, BC.

Mandarte Island

My Master of Science (MSc) program on the nesting biology of Glaucous-winged Gulls began in September 1960 and ended May 1963. The fieldwork for that program was conducted on Mandarte Island, a small, rocky island, about seven hundred metres long and one hundred metres wide in Haro Strait, about nine kilometres from Sidney, the nearest town on Vancouver Island. The fieldwork consisted of four months each, from May 1 until August 31 in 1961 and 1962. My companion was Frank Tompa, a refugee from the 1956 Hungarian Revolution, who conducted a population study of Song Sparrows.

There were two cabins on the island, one built in the style of a Hungarian hunting cabin, which served as sleeping quarters, and the other was the kitchen. The builder of the sleeping cabin was Joseph Takacs, another refugee from the Hungarian Revolution. Joseph was the assistant of Gerry van Tets, a Dutch Canadian, who pioneered seabird research on Mandarte Island in 1957. Gerry and Joseph collected driftwood from Mandarte and nearby islands to build the cabins.

Gerry studied the behaviour of Doubled-crested and Pelagic Cormorants from 1957 to 1959. In 1959, Gerry was joined by Rudi Drent, who studied the breeding biology of Pigeon Guillemots in 1959 and 1960. Rudi, also of Dutch origin, helped me start the third seabird study on Mandarte, the breeding biology of Glaucous-winged Gulls. Dr. Miklos Udvardy, who hailed from Hungary, supervised the studies of Rudi, Frank, and me. The beginning of the Mandarte bird research therefore had a distinct Dutch-Hungarian flavour.

Bare rock and grass were interspersed with a few trees and mostly shrubs wherever there was sufficient soil on Mandarte Island. In May, Camas lilies bloomed and added a touch of blue to grassy patches. Mandarte is a First Nations reserve and aboriginal peoples harvested the edible Camas bulbs in the past. Besides Camas bulbs, they also harvested gull eggs. During one incident, they collected gull eggs that I had marked with numbers to determine the time interval the eggs were laid in one of my study plots. They later came to our cabin with a dozen marked eggs and asked what the numbers meant. I explained these were part of a gull study. It did not bother me that they had taken the marked eggs, as it was their island and the eggs presented only a small part of my study. I asked them to share coffee with us, to which they agreed.

About 5,500 seabirds nested on Mandarte Island each year, of which Glaucous-winged Gulls were by far the most numerous. The gulls nested mostly in grassy areas and on bare rocks, while Double-crested and Pelagic Cormorants occupied rocky ledges on the western cliffside of Mandarte. Pigeon Guillemot nests were dispersed in rock cavities. A few Tufted Puffins nested in rocky burrows, and one or two pairs of Black Oystercatchers laid their eggs in little rock depressions just above the high tide line.

Passerine birds also nested on the island. Song Sparrows and Northwestern Crows were the most numerous passerine birds, and nested all over the island. A pair of Barn Swallows began to nest on the island on the roof beam in our kitchen when I began my study. We left the kitchen door open to provide access for the swallows to their nest. When the eggs hatched, the swallows began to dive-bomb us. To avoid disturbing them, we minimized our use of the kitchen.

Frank and I were the sole occupants of Mandarte, except for a few occasional guests. I enjoyed Frank's meals, which were prepared with a generous dose of red paprika. During the day, we hardly saw each other, as we often conducted our research at different parts of the island from early in the morning until evening. We were so busy with our research that we never became bored. At night, we shared dinner in the kitchen, or, if the weather permitted, at a small table in front of the cabin. That was when we discussed our past experiences such as World War II, the Hungarian Revolution, student life, and political events, while enjoying a great view over Haro Strait. When the Anacortes-Sidney ferry passed by the island in the evening, we waved at the ferry with a Coleman lamp, and those aboard the ferry responded with a horn blast while announcing to the passengers what we did. At night, we slept well after long days of fieldwork, the waves lapping against the rocky shores below our cabin.

Once a week, we prepared our boat and outboard motor for a trip to North Saanich and Sidney to obtain provisions. In North Saanich, we would visit the Mathews at Randle's Landing, where we obtained our supply of drinking water and each had our weekly shower. After the showers, the Mathews invited us for lunch, during which we discussed the latest world events, as we did not know what was going on beyond Mandarte.

In Sidney, we bought freshly baked bread, with its irresistible aroma, from the Sidney Bakery. As soon as we left the bakery, we broke huge chunks of it and devoured the bread on the spot. That is what island life does to you when you live on a small rock in the sea! One week we forgot to buy butter, and ate bread without it. That incident established a lifelong habit for me. I no longer eat bread with butter or margarine.

The next stop was at a small grocery store called Cash & Carry, belonging to Wilkie and Winnie Gardner, who not infrequently invited us for dinner. Frank, who loved books, spent time in Cornish Bookstore, which resulted in dinners with the Cornishes. When invited for dinner, we returned to Mandarte late at night from Sidney wharf at Beacon Avenue by boat. On warm August nights, the waves created by our boat set off beautiful green fireworks because of the presence of light-emitting Noctiluca in the sea.

At the post office, we picked up our mail, where we were welcomed as the birdie boys. In short, we felt part of the Sidney community. The mail collection was a highlight for us. I recall one particular day in 1961, when I received my exam marks from the University of British Columbia. It was on July 14, my birthday, and when I opened the letter, I read that my exam average rated first class. It was the best birthday present for a long time, as my undergraduate exam average was usually below that. It showed that motivation paid off.

Each month there was a particular day when the tide was at its lowest. That day we called Abalone Day, as abalones would be within our reach. We removed them with a pocketknife from the rock surface. Frank would cook the abalone first in seawater and remove the shells; after that he would pound them with a piece of driftwood to make them tender. After frying, the abalone was delicious. Our supervisor, Miklos Udvardy, would try to time his visits to us on Abalone Day.

One day in 1962, Miklos brought along a visitor. It was David Lack, a prominent avian ecologist from the Edward Grey Institute of Field Ornithology in Oxford, England. By sheer coincidence, I was testing David Lack's hypothesis that the clutch size of birds had been adapted by natural selection to correspond to the largest number of young that parents can raise. I had added gull chicks to normal broods of three chicks or less. Lack predicted that the gulls would not be able to raise more than three chicks. Later in the season, it turned out the gulls were able to raise families of four, five, or even six young successfully. Lack was so worried about my results that he wrote to me a year and a half later about how he could save his clutch size hypothesis (see Part IV—David Lack's letter and Ron Ydenberg's Tribute).

One weekend when I was alone on the island, Dr. Clifford Carl, the director of the British Columbia Provincial Museum in Victoria, and his wife visited the island unexpectedly with their houseboat. At the time of their visit, I was doing fieldwork. As it was very hot, I walked in my underwear and wore a hard hat to which I taped a stick, which protruded like an antenna, to prevent aggressive parent gulls from striking my head with their feet while I was checking their young. When the Carls saw me in that unique attire, they must have thought something was wrong with me, as they asked if I was all right. They invited me to their boat for a meal, and looked relieved when I seemed normal. Clifford Carl proved to be of great help later, as he invited me to publish my MSc thesis in its entirety in the Occasional Papers of the British Columbia Provincial Museum. It was my first published work, and although the Occasional Papers Series were relatively obscure, my published thesis became a Citation Classic (see Part IV—This Week's Citation Classic).

In August, the young gulls obtained their first flight. My fieldwork, which I had enjoyed immensely, was coming to an end. By the end of August, Frank and I had locked up the cabins and packed our belongings. We parked our boat and engine at Randle's Landing and travelled by ferry to the mainland. We looked forward to meeting our friends at university, whom we had not seen in four months.

Immigrant Gone to Heaven

Cabins on Mandarte Island, early spring 1962.
Kitchen(L); Sleeping cabin (R); The cabins were my sole residence for eight months in 1961 and 1962. I shared them with Frank Tompa, a fellow graduate student.

Mandarte Island, Summer 1962. Dining table in front of cabin. Primitive as it looks, the dining table was pivotal to sharing field observations, World War II experiences, scientific discoveries, and political events. We entertained visiting bird watchers, fellow graduate students, friends, and ornithologists, among them David Lack of the Edward Grey Institute of Field Ornithology at Oxford University, England.

Mandarte Island, Summer 1962. Gulls on nesting territories. Gulls, which I trapped, banded, and colour-coded at their nests, were observed at the Vancouver City dump 67 km away. They returned to the island either on the same or the following day to feed their young. One colour-banded pair was later observed to maintain a winter territory along the Stanley Park shore in Vancouver. This was the first evidence that nesting mates remained together beyond the breeding season.

Mandarte Island, Summer 1962. Cormorants nesting on rock ledges; Halibut Island (forefront).

Goodbye MSc, Hello PhD

I prepared my Master of Science (MSc) thesis during my last session at the University of British Columbia from September 1962 to May 1963. The fieldwork had been done previously on Mandarte Island. During that last winter, I taught first year zoology students two afternoons a week and attended university seminars. That left sufficient time to write my thesis.

I worked many hours on the thesis and sometimes forgot the time of day. I walked the streets at night for a rest from the paperwork. Once, police stopped me and asked what I was doing that late on the street. I told them I was taking a break from writing my thesis, and lived a few blocks away. When the police looked suspicious, I showed them where I lived. They checked my residence, which had handwritten pages and notes strewn over the chairs, table, floor, and bed. Confronted by the mess of paper, they wished me good luck.

I presented the final thesis to my supervising committee in April 1963. The thesis title was "The Breeding Ecology of the Glaucous-winged Gull on Mandarte Island, BC." My supervisor, Miklos Udvardy, was surprised that my study was mainly on the ecology, and to a lesser extent on the behaviour of gulls. I had told him before what the subject of my study was, but somehow it just did not sink in. Nevertheless, after some deliberations, he settled for the final product and was proud of what I had produced. My oral thesis defence took place during the second week in May, which I passed with flying colours. When the committee congratulated me on my successful research, I felt happy with what I had accomplished.

After I finished my thesis defense, there were no friends to share the news with, as they had moved on to summer jobs. I therefore visited my former landlady, Mrs. Florence Bradshaw, with whom I boarded during my undergraduate years at university. Florence was happy to see me, and congratulated me. She had just sold her house, because it had become too much work to maintain. I said farewell, and that was the last time I saw Florence.

I cleaned my rented basement suite and packed my belongings. I planned to leave Vancouver the next day by train for Edmonton, Alberta, where I had accepted a summer student job with the Canadian Wildlife Service (CWS). After my CWS summer job, I planned to attend the University of Alberta as a PhD student.

That evening, I went to a movie that turned to be a classic, called *Lawrence of Arabia*. The movie took my mind off any lingering academic thoughts. The next morning, I bade farewell to my landlord, and took a taxi to the train station. After one day and night on the train, I reached Edmonton. A CWS staff member picked me up from the train station and brought me to a motel, where I stayed for the next few weeks. I did not know it at the time, but Edmonton would be my city of residence for the next twelve years. I held two different jobs with the CWS that summer. In the first one, I had to assist a limnologist with collecting water samples from prairie potholes in Saskatchewan. The second one consisted of investigating the food habits of ducks. Both jobs lasted two months each. Both the limnologist and biologist were nice, dedicated fellows, but the limnologist, called Dudley, was difficult to work with. For example, if we sampled a pothole located in a meadow with a closed cattle gate, it had to be opened his way. Although I had opened hundreds or perhaps thousands of cattle gates before, Dudley's detailed instructions for a simple operation drove me crazy. After a while, I asked Dudley to open the gate himself, as I could not stand it any longer, to which he agreed.

After working hours, Dudley took me to gravel and rock pits, where we sorted through small rocks for hours, as he was interested in collecting semiprecious stones. He polished those stones at home. He also collected leeches in the evenings for a university professor who was a leech specialist, but had gone mad. I did not mind those off-duty activities at all. Dudley invited me once to his home for dinner with his wife and daughter, which I enjoyed. However, I was aghast to see rock piles beneath tables, in corners, and underneath beds.

As I had gained sufficient experience with cattle gates, water samples, rock piles, and leeches, I asked the CWS director if I could do something else. My request was granted, and to Dudley's disappointment, I was transferred to Lawson Sugden, who studied the diet of ducklings near Strathmore in southern Alberta. I got along well with Lawson, although the working conditions left much to be desired. Early in the morning (between four and five o'clock), we left our motel and collected ducklings from potholes and marshes, to minimize upsetting farmers. It was not something I enjoyed, but it was part of the research. On the plus side, Lawson's data contributed to understanding what makes a good rearing habitat for ducklings, and ultimately, helped preserve that habitat.

In the motel, we dissected the ducklings and preserved their stomach contents. My motel room, which unfortunately was used for dissection, stank to high heavens. Lawson, who was deaf, had the TV at high volume so he could hear the reporter's comments on his favourite ice hockey games. After dissection, we cleaned up the room and went for breakfast, for which by then, I had lost my appetite. After six weeks of fieldwork, we left for Edmonton where I processed and analyzed the food samples in the laboratory.

In Edmonton, I received a letter from my former supervisor, Miklos Udvardy, at the University of British Columbia. He enclosed a letter from Dr. Niko Tinbergen, who offered me to conduct a PhD study in Oxford, England, under his supervision. I felt honoured, as Tinbergen was well known for his studies on gull behaviour and was a Nobel Prize winner. Miklos urged me to accept Tinbergen's offer. However, for practical reasons, I decided to go on with my plans to conduct a PhD study at the University of Alberta.

With Lawson, I scouted for a location where I could conduct field studies for my PhD. I found one not far from Edmonton, at Miquelon Lake, where two species of gulls nested: California and Ring-billed Gulls.

After I finished my CWS summer job, I had sufficient funds to buy a car. I had never owned a car before, and bought a new Volkswagen for two thousand dollars. I was happy with my little red Beetle, which now became my main source of transport. In the fall of 1963, I often drove to Miquelon Lake, which bordered a Provincial Park. I befriended John Erickson, the park manager, and his wife, Babs, at whose home I was always welcome. I also bought a small boat and outboard motor, which helped me access the lake islands where the gulls nested in spring and summer. With the help of my long-time friends, Jack Boulogne and Carl Dietz, I built a small cabin on one island, which served as my observation and living quarters. I looked very much forward to the following May, when my field research would commence at Miquelon Lake.

Observation cabin and living quarters, Miquelon Lake, Spring 1965. Sleeping room upstairs; kitchen downstairs.
This picture was taken when the lake was still frozen. During ice breakup, I was marooned on the island for one week. During that time, Canada Geese provided some comic entertainment. The geese would land on the lake and slide for long distances over the ice. Sometimes a gander landed in front of his mate on the ice, but could not stop sliding. To prevent crashing into his mate, the gander would jump up and somersault over her, after which he crash-landed and rolled like a barrel over the ice before coming to a stop. Not even Russian circus clowns could equal that performance.

Immigrant Gone to Heaven

Ring-billed Gulls nesting at Miquelon Lake.

Finishing my PhD

I finished the fieldwork on the breeding biology of California and Ring-billed Gulls at Miquelon Lake for my PhD program at the University of Alberta in the summer of 1965. In September of that year, I took up residence in Athabasca Hall on the university campus. Since meals were now provided at the university cafeteria, I had more time to spend on my studies. Most of my time went into preparing for a comprehensive oral exam on my knowledge of zoology, which all PhD students had to pass before continuing their program. I went through many basic and advanced zoology textbooks and journals to keep abreast of the latest research. I read books from cover to cover and underlined all pertinent information to which there seemed to be no end. In March 1966, I was notified that I had to take my comprehensive exam within a few days. The PhD student who just preceded me failed the exam, which was not encouraging news. When the day of the exam arrived, I had a bad case of flu, which made me feel drowsy and indifferent. One professor told me after the exam that that was a good state to be in, because most students were nervous during the comprehensive exam. When I entered the examination room, there were nine professors representing various disciplines in zoology seated around a long rectangular table. They intently stared at me, perhaps looking forward to another slaughter. One of them threw snippets of skeletons of marine invertebrates at me, consisting of abalones, chitons, starfish, sea snails, sea cucumbers, and sea urchins. He asked me to identify the animals they represented and describe their anatomy, classification, and how and where they lived. Since I had previously spent two summers on Mandarte Island, where I frequently examined the marine fauna in small tidal pools and along the seashore, I recognized the snippets immediately. I indifferently tossed them back to my interrogator, while describing them in detail. My examiners looked surprised, as marine invertebrates were not supposed to be my field of expertise.

Another professor asked me to draw the digestive tract of an Acanthocephala worm. I replied there was no such thing, which was the correct answer. After a few more trick questions, they stood up and congratulated me. When the other zoology graduate students heard the news that I had passed my comprehensive, they cheered and congratulated me.

After the comprehensive exam, I felt relaxed, and had time to socialize with friends and students at Athabasca Hall. Many of them hailed from different countries, which made an interesting mix of foreign backgrounds. The past winter had been very cold with a wind chill factor up to minus sixty-seven degrees Celsius, which meant that few students left Athabasca Hall, except when dressed in insulated parkas to attend classes. Static electricity built up in the Hall, which meant that if you touched one another, you would get an electric shock. By the end of March, it was no longer that cold, and students built beautiful ice castles on campus. My friend Mohamed Hassan from Zimbabwe, who had not seen ice castles before, and I went out to admire the castles.

In April, I drove with my friend, Hans Vahlquist, a geography student from Sweden, to Miquelon Lake. Hans was intrigued by the Swedish spoken by my friend, John Erickson, the local park warden. Hans told me that John spoke old Swedish, which was spoken in Sweden a hundred years ago. John Erickson hailed from a Swedish settlement near Miquelon Lake, where his ancestors pioneered.

Sometime in April, Dr. Ward Stevens, the CWS Director in Edmonton, phoned and asked if there were any foreign movies shown at the campus theatre. I told him there was one, and he expressed interest to see the movie. When Ward arrived, the theatre was packed, and we took the last seats at the back. Sometime during the intermission, Ward struggled to retrieve some papers from his back pocket, which he asked me to sign. I asked what they were, and he said they were application forms for a CWS biologist job in Edmonton. After signing, I asked when the job interview would take place. Ward informed me that this was the interview and I had passed.

The movie was lousy and the hero committed suicide, but the employment offer was great news. It was also timely, as a few days later, my PhD supervisor informed me that he no longer had grants to further support my study. He looked surprised when I smiled at the bad news. I did not tell him the reason.

My CWS job would start on July 1, 1966. After leaving Athabasca Hall in early May, I looked for a place to rent near the CWS office. I found an apartment on the tenth floor of Rowand House, with a beautiful view over the North Saskatchewan River. I loved the apartment, which would be my residence until the fall of 1968.

My new CWS director was John Kelsall, as Ward Stevens was on a two-year leave in Malaysia. My new supervisor was Ron Mackay. Both John and Ron knew that I still had to write my PhD thesis. They gave me time to work on my thesis. I loved my first year with CWS; my new colleagues were easy to get along with, and some of them became friends. In September 1967, I passed my PhD thesis defense successfully. This was another milestone in my life. Not long after my defense, I left for a vacation in Holland to celebrate my PhD status with family and friends. One of my friends living in the Netherlands was Rudi Drent, who had invited me to visit him on Mandarte Island in 1960. That visit had sparked my career as an avian biologist. Rudi now studied at the University of Groningen for his Doctor of Science degree. In 1966, I had visited Rudi in Groningen. We then travelled to Schiermonnikoog, where Rudi conducted his field studies. There we made a detailed list of all the birds we observed, as Rudi was also an ardent birdwatcher. While I was there, Rudi provided excellent advice on my thesis in progress.

When Rudi arrived at my mother's residence in Gorinchem in 1967, he congratulated me on getting my PhD, after which we talked nonstop in my mother's drawing room about our bird studies, while family peeped around the corner of the door from time to time to see what was going on. After the whole family was present in the living room, Rudi and I joined them.

Later in the evening, we were joined by Gerry van Tets, who pioneered the seabird studies on Mandarte Island. Gerry happened to be at The Hague from Australia, where he was employed as a government scientist. When Gerry entered the crowded living room, he presented a bouquet of roses to Berta, my sister-in-law, who he mistook for my mother.

After the celebration, my family left. Adrian, my brother-in-law, drove Rudi, Gerry, and me to the Arkelpoort, where the three of us got off and walked to the Langedijk, where Rudi would stay for the night at my sister Cato's place. Rudi planned to leave for Groningen early the next morning. During our walk through downtown Gorinchem, the three of us excitedly discussed future research plans. After dropping off Rudi at the Langedijk, Gerry and I marched like soldiers down the middle of the dark streets of Gorinchem to the train station, where Gerry boarded the train just in time for The Hague. That was the last time I saw Gerry. Celebrating my PhD degree with Rudi and Gerry, who, like me, had started their seabird research on the same small Island in British Columbia, was an event I will never forget.

Publication of PhD thesis, Canadian Wildlife Service, 1970.

Wedding at Lunch Break

Shortly after I had finished my PhD thesis defense in September 1967, I went for lunch at the University Student Union cafeteria in Edmonton. While picking up my food tray, I noticed two girls at a table. One was tall and blond, and the other short and lively. I took a seat opposite the lively one and introduced myself, showing my student ID card. They did likewise. During the ensuing conversation, the charms of the lively one did not escape me. Her name was Rebecca and she hailed from the Philippines. I phoned her later and invited her for dinner, to which she agreed. We learned more about each other over dinner. Afterward, I sent her a bouquet of roses at Pembina Hall on the university campus where she lived. Her tall blond friend, Erika, warned her that I meant serious business and to be careful, to which Rebecca replied: "Do not worry; that's the last man I ever want to marry."

Shortly after sending Rebecca the flowers, I left for a vacation in Holland to celebrate my PhD with my family. After my return from Holland, there was a noisy party in the suite above me in Rowand House. The noise kept me awake for hours but stopped when I hit the ceiling with a broomstick. I later heard from Rebecca that she had attended that party.

I called Rebecca the next day and invited her to see a movie, but she said she was busy with her studies. I repeated my phone call a week later, but with the same result. I therefore told her I would not call again if she was not interested in continuing our friendship. Later, she went with her friend Leona to Stettler to spend Christmas with Leona's family. Shortly after Christmas, Rebecca returned to Pembina Hall. All her friends had left and she felt very lonely. She called and asked if I was still interested in taking her out. I was, and we had a great time together, after which our relationship changed for the better.

Early in January, I had a bad case of the flu and Rebecca looked after me in Rowand House. In February, we decided to get married. Rebecca wanted to get married in a church; however, I had not been in a church for many years and was reluctant to go back. Rebecca, who was Roman Catholic, asked me to contact a priest, which I did. The priest demanded that I go to catechism for three months before getting married. He told me our children should be instructed in the Roman Catholic faith. I told him I would not be a party to a deal like that and our conversation ended there. Rebecca heard what the priest demanded and understood my response, but asked to try once more with the bishop. I immediately walked to the nearest phone booth to phone the bishop and explain my dilemma. The bishop disagreed with the priest and laughed. He told me to get married and be happy. I was happy with the bishop's reply, and we decided to get married at the Bureau of Vital Statistics.

On February 20, 1968, the day we planned to marry, Rebecca and I drove my red Volkswagen to the Canadian Wildlife Service office where I met my supervisor, Ron Mackay. I was supposed to give a lecture on some aspects of my work to provincial biologists that day, and Ron asked me if I was ready to proceed. I informed Ron I was not going to give the lecture. Ron looked shocked and said I needed a good reason not to go through with it. I said I had, and told him I was getting married in half an hour, and wanted him to be my best man at our wedding at the Bureau of Vital Statistics. Ron was flabbergasted, but agreed when I informed him my wife-to-be was waiting in my Volkswagen. I picked up Mike, another surprised colleague, to be our second witness and off we drove to the bureau. A pile of snow blocked the entrance to the bureau, but nothing could stop us now, and we climbed over it. The ceremony was simple and beautiful and was finished in fifteen minutes; what more can you ask for a wedding? I drove Ron and Mike back to the office, after which Rebecca and I went to a restaurant called Zorba the Greek. It was in a dark basement where we groped our way to a table and shared a pizza for lunch. After lunch, I brought Rebecca to her chemistry laboratory classroom at the university where she taught first-year students. When a student asked her a question and addressed her as Miss Arrieta, she told the class she had just changed her name to Mrs. Vermeer during lunch break.

In the meantime, I returned to my office, where it was announced over the intercom that I had just gotten married. My colleagues were surprised, as none of them knew of my intention to get married. I invited everyone to celebrate my wedding at the beer parlour. Everybody walked out of the office to the nearest parlour and celebrated the surprise event of the day. Nobody went back to work that afternoon.

After leaving the parlour, I picked up Rebecca from university from where we drove to Rowand House, our new abode. Late in the evening, I phoned my mother in Holland, who was having breakfast, and told her I had just gotten married. She answered: "Kees, married? Unbelievable! We all looked forward to your wedding here in Holland." I told her it was too late for that, after which I introduced her to Rebecca, who said in a few Dutch words: *Hallo moeder, ik ben Rebecca.*

The next morning, we shopped for furniture: within one hour we spent every cent I had saved during the last two years. I learned for the first time that Rebecca loved shopping, testing my frugal lifestyle. I also had to adjust to a new diet—instead of ham and eggs, we ate canned peaches for breakfast. Goodbye potatoes and steaks; hello rice, noodle soup, and chicken. I found out life was no bowl of cherries, but rather a can of peaches; I was happy anyway.

Shortly after our wedding, we invited all our university friends to our apartment for a party. They came in droves and brought their guitars, drums, and other musical instruments. We barbequed one chicken after another on a rotisserie on the balcony, as there was no space in the kitchen. We ate and sang until late in the evening. At five o'clock in the morning, Rebecca woke up and asked me to buy grapes, because she no longer wanted canned peaches for breakfast. I asked her if she could at least wait until the stores were open, to which she agreed. I then realized, although I had a PhD in Zoology, there was still much to learn about the behaviour of female Homo sapiens.

Rebecca at Pembina Hall, University of Alberta, Edmonton, Christmas 1967.

Rebecca in a park near our apartment in Edmonton, March 1968.

PART II
Life of an Ornithologist

From the Polder to Canada's Prairies and Pacific Coast

My career as a CWS biologist and ornithologist began in Edmonton, Alberta on July 1, 1966. It was my first permanent job since I arrived in Canada as a Dutch migrant in 1954. I moved from a University of Alberta campus residence to a downtown apartment to be closer to my new workplace. As my PhD thesis was in progress, I was allowed time to complete it while conducting CWS assignments.

On February 20, 1968, I married Rebecca, who moved in with me at my downtown apartment. In October, we bought a house in Sherwood Park, a suburb of Edmonton. My job as a biologist, and later as a research scientist in Edmonton, lasted nine years.

In 1975, I transferred from Edmonton to a CWS office on Westham Island near Ladner in British Columbia. We bought a house in North Saanich near the town of Sidney on Vancouver Island, as I had fond memories of shopping for groceries and getting mail in Sidney in 1961 and 1962. During those years, I conducted research for an MSc degree on the biology of Glaucous-winged Gulls nesting on a small islet, called Mandarte Island. From Mandarte, I travelled by boat to Sidney.

From the time of our arrival in British Columbia, I travelled by ferry between Sidney and Tsawwassen, and from there to my CWS office. After riding the ferry for two years, I became a guest scientist at the Institute of Ocean Sciences. The Institute is a few kilometers from my home on the Saanich peninsula. From then on, I visited my CWS office only when necessary.

This part of my story has ten chapters. Some are about family and others are work-related stories, and some are both. The first chapter "Roaming the Dutch Polder" describes how and where I acquired my interest in birds in the Netherlands. Two chapters, "Pleas for Protection of Fish-eating Bird Colonies" and "Pursuing the Trail of Pesticides and Mercury in Aquatic Birds" were previously published in *Blue Jay, Winter 2018, Volume 76.4* and *Spring 2019, Volume 77.1,* respectively. Although the format varies, and chapters were written at different times and circumstances, they nevertheless provide a glimpse of my life as a CWS biologist and ornithologist. Biologists come from all walks of life. What they have in common is that they care about or are interested in life-forms other than humans. The world needs more biologists to assess and warn humanity of its increasing negative effects on many of those life-forms.

Roaming the Dutch Polder

I do not remember the exact age I became first interested in birds, but it might have been when I was about seven, and lived in a place called Noordeloos, where my father was a school principal. It was, and still is, a picturesque village in the Alblasserwaard that is split in half by a meandering stream, called a boezem. We had a large garden with flowers, vegetables, strawberries, berry bushes, and fruit trees. A variety of birds visited our garden, such as the Great Tit, Chaffinch, Robin, Blackbird, Wren, House Sparrow, and occasionally, a Green Woodpecker. At the front of our house, a pair of House Martins had their nest cemented to the wall underneath the awning of our roof. At nearby farms, Barn Swallows fed their young in clay nests built on barn ledges, and a handsome pair of White Storks nested on a wagon wheel on a high wooden pole. In the boezem, Coots and Moorhens swam along the shore and visited their nests in reed beds, while Herons stalked fishes along the water's edge.

When my family moved to Gorinchem in 1938, my interest in birds continued. At that time, our house on the Emmastraat was on the edge of the polder. But it was not until World War II that I explored the polder with my friend Sjors from 1942 through 1944. We did not continue into 1945, as much of the polder had been flooded during the previous autumn on orders of the German occupation forces to obstruct the advance of the Allied Liberation Army. Shortly after the inundation of the polder, large numbers of waterbirds invaded the newly created marshes. I then wished I possessed a small boat for entering this new waterbird haven. The flooded polder did not stop the Allied Forces, as its soldiers suddenly arrived at our doorstep on the morning of May 5, 1945. Shortly after, German troops in Gorinchem surrendered in massive numbers to a few Allied soldiers.

During our polder explorations, Sjors and I jumped across ditches with the aid of a long pole. Two of the most common meadow birds nesting in the polder were Black-tailed Godwits and Lapwings. The Godwit is a tall and handsome bird with a long bill. Its clear call could be heard almost anywhere. They nested in tall grass and laid four large pear-shaped, olive-green eggs. Lapwings nested mostly on arable land, but also on meadows with short grass. Like the Godwit, they produced clutches of four eggs, but there was no discernable nest, just a scrape or a small dip in the ground. Of all birds, we were most interested in finding the nests of Mallards, as their eggs were a substitute for chicken eggs. The latter were a coveted commodity during the occupation period. Mallards nested both on the ground and in pollard willows, where they can be readily located.

Importance of the Knotwilg (Pollard Willow) for Nesting Birds

I use the Dutch word *knotwilg* instead of pollard willow, as it is the most characteristic tree of the Dutch polder landscape. Another reason is my sentimental attachment to the knotwilg as a symbol of defiance and redemption. A knotwilg is an ordinary willow tree that is sawed off at a height of two meters a few years after planting. After that, the branches, which grow as a bush from its knot, or "head," are cut every five to seven years. The branches were used in the past to make baskets and other household items. The head is formed as a result of the thickening of the base of the branches and is a response to the trauma caused to the willow by the cutting. However, there is a redeeming feature of the trauma caused by man to the willow tree, and that is that its head has become a nesting refuge for many wild birds in the open polder.

The knotwilg head becomes larger with age. When the knotwilg grows old, the head starts to decay from the inside. Songbirds begin to nest in its cracks and cavities. With further decay, a bowl with humus-rich soil forms in the head. Windblown seeds and spores sprout there, and the knotwilg bowl will acquire its own microflora, such as grasses, stinging nettles, bitterroot, and oak ferns. At this stage, a Crow or Mallard may nest in the bowl. With further decay, the bowl begins to sag, until it drops down halfway inside the old and now hollow trunk. Owls, which avoid daylight, start nesting deep in the hollow trunk, while a Stock Dove, which nests in cavities, enters the hollow willow through an opening in the side of its trunk.

Collection of Mallard Eggs

Mallards commonly nest in knotwilgen growing along ditches. A single or a pair of ducks swimming in a ditch near a knotwilg could be a sign that they nest nearby. We climbed a tree if there were signs of down feathers. If a nest was present, we checked one of the eggs to see if it was fresh or incubated by holding it in water. If the egg floated, it was incubated and we returned the egg to the nest, and left the hen who almost always would return in peace. If the egg sank, it was fresh and we would take all of the eggs if there were enough of them to make it worthwhile; if there were only few, we would leave them. A successive visit depended on the next time we had a chance to visit; if that was several weeks later, there was no point in returning, as all eggs would be incubated by that time. We therefore practised a type of conservation which we thought was the right thing to do.

The trips into the polder were much more about fun, and little about economic necessity. Although we jumped across many ditches and climbed many trees, we only found two or three nests every spring. Moreover, Sjors and I shared the eggs, regardless of who found the nest, leaving us half of the bounty each (about six eggs per year). We always visited the polder with great expectation to find a nest; and when we did, there was great excitement! Back at home, we proudly displayed the eggs on the dinner table for the whole family to admire.

Other Birds Nesting in Knotwilgen

By searching for Mallard nests, we came across Crows and Kestrels nesting in knotwilg bowls. Crows are wary and spot you early. Their alarm calls grow increasingly raucous if you come close. Kestrels are small diurnal raptors and produce clutches of two brown, beautifully speckled eggs. Kestrels are common in the polder throughout the year, and hover in the sky from where they spot their prey.

On several occasions, I surprised large Long-eared Owls on their nest deep down in the hollow knotwilg trunks. The surprise was mutual, as the owls would make much noise trying to scramble up along the inside of the willow trunk to the surface. I had to get out of their way quickly as they would brush against me in their haste to escape. They would settle on branches only a few feet away and stare at me with their large and beautiful orange-yellow eyes. I would climb down in a hurry, as I did not want to further disturb those magnificent birds. Once I surprised a Little Owl, a much smaller bird than the Long-eared Owl, on its nest with beautiful and almost round white eggs deep inside a willow trunk. The beautiful Redstart is the most common songbird nesting in knotwilg cavities. Cycling through the polder in spring, one can hear Redstarts singing from willow branches everywhere.

Black-tailed Godwit, national bird of the Netherlands. (Photo Credit: AdobeStock 157 343004).

Lapwing.
(Photo Credit: AdobeStock 104 131394).

Dutch polder and knotwilgen.
(Photo Credit: AdobeStock 337 59150).

**Little Owl in knotwilg Cavity.
(Photo Credit: AdobeStock 258 397868).**

Polder as Refuge

Besides trekking through the polder for adventure, enjoyment, and necessity, there was another important reason for my visits. The polder was a refuge when I needed to get away from people, and from the goings-on of German occupation of Holland. The polder visits lifted my spirit. One bird in particular helped me do that during the dark days of war: it was the song of the Skylark.

In 2010, my wife and I visited Auschwitz-Birkenau in Poland. At the end of our concentration camp walk, I felt heavy-hearted. Then, suddenly, there was the uplifting and uninterrupted song of a Skylark rising steeply to the Auschwitz sky, and the burden fell away. No matter the amount of human misery, Skylarks will keep singing, as Lieutenant Colonel John McCrae recorded in his World War I poem, "In Flanders fields … and in the sky, the larks still bravely singing, fly."

Skylarks may affect people in different ways. To the poet Shelley, they were inspiring; to me, they lifted my spirit in wartime. I wonder what they meant to Auschwitz victims.

Ten species of larks occur in Europe, of which three nest in Holland and Flanders: the Crested Lark, Wood Lark, and Skylark. The Crested Lark hardly sings during flight, but sings mostly on the ground or from a rooftop. The Wood Lark, a rather shy bird, has a brief and unremarkable song during flight; and sings mostly from the top of a shrub or tree. Only the Skylark sings almost exclusively during its long flight. Therefore, there is no doubt in my mind that the word "larks" McCrae mentioned in his poem refers to the Skylark.

For readers in the Netherlands, I enclose a copy of McCrae's poem, "In Flanders Fields," as they may not be familiar with it. The Netherlands was not a WWI participant.

In Flanders Fields

In Flanders fields the poppies blow
Between the crosses row on row,
That mark our place; and in the sky
The larks, still bravely singing, fly
Scarce heard amid the guns below.
We are the dead. Short days ago
We lived, felt dawn, saw sunset glow,
Loved, and were loved, and now we lie
In Flanders fields.
Take up our quarrel with the foe:
To you from failing hands, we throw
The torch; be yours to hold it high.
If ye break faith with us who die
We shall not sleep, though poppies grow
In Flanders fields.

By Lieutenant Colonel John McCrae

First Years of Marriage

After our brief marriage ceremony at the Bureau of Vital Statistics on February 20, 1968, Rebecca and I returned to conventional life. Rebecca was enrolled in a Master of Science program in Physical Chemistry at the University of Alberta, Edmonton. I documented nesting populations of cormorants, herons and pelicans, while employed by the Canadian Wildlife Service. Rebecca and I loved the outdoors. We traveled to Miquelon Lake, where I had studied gulls for my PhD; to New Norway, where I made observations of a Great Blue Heron colony on the Battle River, and where we had picnics with friends later on; to Dowling and Newell lakes where I investigated nesting Canada Geese; to Writing-on-Stone Provincial Park on the Milk River, which is known for its petroglyphs, and birds not seen anywhere else in the province; to the St. Paul and Lac La Biche lake region, where we fished and picked blueberries; and to the Rocky Mountains in Jasper National Park, where we enjoyed the spectacular scenery and watched elk, moose, and bighorn sheep.

I mixed work with pleasure, and often took Rebecca along during my fieldwork. We fished on weekends; the fish we caught were mostly pike, but also perch and pickerel. Once while we filleted pike at the bank of Eleanor Lake, a black bear appeared out of the bush. We tried to shoo the bear away, but to no avail. We abandoned the pike and jumped into our boat in the nick of time. We did not mind the bear taking the filleted pike, as there were many more in the lake. As pike was not our favourite fish, we had more fun fishing than eating them.

In the area we fished there were abandoned homesteads with raspberries still growing in old vegetable gardens. We loved eating the juicy and delicious berries which were there for the picking. We filled many buckets to take home. At Lac La Biche, we picked blueberries on a sandy hill infested with blackflies, which took square bites out of exposed skin on wrists, ankles and necks. We put up with the bites, because our love for blueberries was stronger than the discomfort caused by the flies. To this day, Rebecca processes blueberries into her signature low-sugar blueberry jam with lime. Many of the jars are shared with friends who love her jam.

In September, we travelled to Holland to introduce Rebecca to my mother and family, and to have a late honeymoon. My family was curious about Rebecca, who was the first foreigner to marry into the Vermeer family. We stayed with my mother at my old residence in the Emmastraat in Gorinchem. I felt happy to be in the old house again, although it was for the last time. That house held many memories. During World War II, my Emmastraat family worked as a team to survive the German occupation. (Part III—Our Family Adapts to the German Occupation).

We explored Gorinchem and visited the city market, where Rebecca bought squid to make "adobo"—food which she fondly remembered from living in the Philippines. However, her culinary skills were undeveloped at that time. My mother chewed and chewed laboriously with her false teeth, but could not make a dent on the squid which was as tough as shoe leather! Rebecca quickly learned how not to cook squid.

We visited Rotterdam and Amsterdam. In Rotterdam, we made a boat trip through the harbour, which is the largest in Europe. In Amsterdam, we visited the Rijksmuseum, as we both love old Dutch paintings. Rebecca bought prints of the works of Rembrandt, Jan Steen, Avercamp, and Breugel, which still adorn our rooms today. A print by Nicolaes Maes (1634–1693) of *Old Woman Saying Grace* is special to me and hangs above my chair where I eat my "daily bread" in the kitchen. The Rijksmuseum is still one of our favourite places, which we visit each time we are in Holland.

We travelled to Paris by train with a Dutch tourist group. Rebecca and I loved Paris. We visited important historic and tourist sites, and I translated to her what the Dutch guide was saying. In our hotel, we were served breakfast in bed each morning—a huge cup of coffee (Rebecca had tea) with French baguettes and croissants. We had a bizarre experience with the footbath in our room, a feature we had not encountered before. As there was no shower stall or bathtub in the room, nor could we find one on our floor, I precariously balanced myself, standing in the footbath. Rebecca handed over glasses of water with which I washed myself. She took her turn after me. We had fun doing it.

Rebecca met my brother Wim and his wife Eggi toward the end of our holiday, as they had been touring Czechoslovakia at that time. They had the adventure of a lifetime trying to get out of the country when its borders were blockaded by Russian tanks. To the great relief of their children, they finally managed to escape. Wim told a great story of solidarity of the Dutch tourists with the people. On their return, Wim and Eggi, like the rest of the family, met Rebecca for the first time. Eggi was drawn like a magnet to Rebecca, her new twenty-one-year-old sister-in-law. The two got along well and shared many laughs.

After spending a wonderful time in Paris and Holland, we returned to Canada with bags and suitcases overloaded with gifts from Mother, and Rebecca's shopping. Eggi and Wim, who brought us to Schiphol airport, wondered how we would get all our baggage through. I managed by carrying, the heavy brass weights of a wall clock my mother gave us in the inside pockets of my jacket. The airport clerk asked me if I was not feeling well, as I leaned on the counter to support the weights. I was afraid the weights would tear through the thin pocket linings and crash on the floor. It is amazing what men have to endure to support the hobbies of their wives. The Dutch wall clock still hangs in our dining room fifty years later and rings the hours on time. When I look at the clock, I remember Mother, and our visit to her at the Emmastraat.

Buying our First House

In October 1968, Bill, an acquaintance at the CWS office invited Rebecca and me for coffee at his home in Sherwood Park, a suburb of Edmonton, Alberta. Since we were looking for a philadendron plant at a greenhouse in Sherwood Park, we accepted Bill's invitation. After coffee, a real estate agent, who was present at Bill's house, showed us a house for sale on Pine Street. It was a three-bedroom bungalow, and after a fifteen-minute tour through the house, Rebecca and I decided to buy the house. It must have been one of the easiest sales the agent made, because we had no intention to buy a house at that time, but just a plant for $1.60 for our apartment. We bought the house for $18,500 with a $3,000 down payment and a 6 ¾ percent interest rate annually (that same house may presently sell for $500,000). We moved into the house in the second week of November 1968, and lived there until May 30, 1975. We enjoyed living there among friendly neighbours and had no regrets in buying the house.

Arrival of our Daughter, Lotus

In January 1969, Rebecca entered the Edmonton University Hospital to give birth of our baby. I was there when Rebecca had labour pains, but was not allowed to see the actual birth, which I regretted, because Rebecca had asked for my support during her labour. To my disdain, a group of medical students were allowed to witness the birth of our baby instead. After the birth, I was allowed to see our baby daughter, who looked healthy. Rebecca and our daughter stayed in the hospital for a week, during which time Rebecca studied for her semestral exams in chemistry while recuperating and learning to care for our daughter. As it was minus thirty degrees Celsius outside, I made a practice run between Sherwood Park and the hospital to scout for places where we could find shelter in case my car broke down. Fortunately, my VW Beetle kept going the day I picked them up from the hospital.

Rebecca stayed home for a week before returning to university to teach chemistry and to her coursework for a Master of Science in Physical Chemistry. We searched for a name of our daughter; we did not want to name her after relatives. We decided to name her Lotus, after a flower. I took on the night feeding of Lotus as Rebecca was exhausted. I compensated for lack of sleep by locking my office door during lunch time to get some rest. We were fortunate to find a babysitter across the road named Edith, who looked after Lotus while we went to work. After one year with Edith, a neighbour named Betty took over the care of Lotus for two years.

Rebecca and I fondly remember several funny incidents during Lotus's early years. One exceedingly busy Halloween night before Lotus learned to walk, we were handing out candies to hundreds of kids. We had no time to pay attention to Lotus, who was crawling on the floor and watching us giving candies to the kids. When the flow of kids had slowed down, we noticed Lotus had disappeared. After searching, we found her behind a big rocking chair with her face smeared and mouth dripping with liquorice over her clothes. She was very quiet and looked content with a bagful of candies. There was also the mysterious disappearance of small fishes from our aquarium and we were finding fish heads on the floor. The mystery was solved when one day we caught Lotus standing on a chair, with one arm in the aquarium, catching fish and decapitating them with her teeth. Another incident was when she cut the hair of a neighbour's small daughter, named Tammy, which did not go over well with the girl's mother. Lotus was banned from playing with Tammy.

Journey to Holland and London

In September 1970, Rebecca and I made our second journey to Gorinchem in Holland. Nadine, another neighbour across the road, volunteered to look after Lotus while we went on holiday. Since Mother had moved from the Emmastraat in 1969 to live with my sister Cato on the Langedijk, we stayed there as well. Mother was happy at the Langedijk, where she had a separate living room fully furnished with her furniture from her home in the Emmastraat. She still cooked her meals, washed dishes, and did her shopping at nearby stores. She regularly fished from the back porch in the Linge harbour. Rebecca joined her, as she loved fishing, too. The two had great fun catching fish, which they threw back into the water as the harbour was polluted.

We travelled to London via the ferry from Hoek van Holland to Harwich. In London we stayed in a bed-and-breakfast. We enjoyed many historic places and buildings in London, but our most memorable event was meeting our Scottish landlady. She served ham and eggs for breakfast, but before we reached that stage, we needed a shower. Early in the morning I knocked on her door to ask where the shower was located. She asked me to open the door. She sat in her bedstead at one side of the large room, and pointed to a bathroom on the other side. There was no shower, only a bathtub. Over the bathtub was a large board with plates and dishes containing butter, sugar, salt, jam, cooking oil, etc, which I removed before entering the tub. While in the tub, I had a pleasant conversation with my landlady sitting in her bedstead at the other end of the room. After my wash, I explained the situation to Rebecca, who took her turn in the tub. When Rebecca expressed her wish to use the tub the next morning, our landlady asked why she wanted to wash again as she had already done so the previous day. To that Rebecca answered, "I can't wake up until I have had my wash."

At breakfast we had a lively conversation about our landlady's experience during WWII. She told us that when London was heavily bombed, she dressed up in her finest clothes and most fashionable shoes and lay down and waited in her bedstead to meet the Lord. But that obviously did not happen, as she lived to tell her story.

Mother's Visit

The year 1971 was particularly eventful for me, because my mother visited our home in Sherwood Park. She had never been outside the Netherlands, and this was her first time travelling by plane. She was eighty-five years old, and was accompanied by my niece, Willy Straatman, when she arrived at the Edmonton airport. She brought fancy porcelain teacups and saucers and little silver spoons, because she could not drink tea or coffee from melmac (plastic) cups, which was all we had. By now, Rebecca had become an experienced cook. There was no shortage of cakes and fine baking, as Rebecca had mastered the *Art of Fine Baking* by Paula Peck, which she had bought from the University Bookstore for ninety-nine cents. However, mother had to get used to the way Rebecca prepared vegetables such as green beans, which were firm and crunchy, and not soft like those in Holland. One highlight was a trip to the Rocky Mountains in Jasper National Park, where we rented a cabin and enjoyed the scenery and wildlife.

In early October, I had to leave Canada for a project to investigate the effects of pesticides on birds in rice fields of Suriname. I said goodbye to my mother, who stayed another two weeks before returning to Holland. It had been a unique and wonderful experience to have her visit Rebecca, Lotus, and me in Canada.

Immigrant Gone to Heaven

Rebecca near the heronry at New Norway, Alberta, 1968.

Kees and Rebecca at Rotterdam Harbour, 1968.

Rebecca, Eggi, and Mother sharing a laugh in Eggi's backyard, Gorinchem, Netherlands, 1968.

Immigrant Gone to Heaven

Mother and Kees in front of our house in Sherwood Park, Alberta, September 1971.

Mother, Lotus, and Rebecca on our patio at Sherwood Park, September 1971.

Pleas for Protection of Fish-eating Bird Colonies

My first job in my Canadian Wildlife Service career in 1966 was to evaluate federal migratory bird sanctuaries in Alberta. With a CWS panel truck, I visited all the sanctuaries and discovered that they were often set up for the wrong reasons, such as to avoid taxes or keep trespassers out. At the end of the evaluation, I concluded that most sanctuaries were not worth keeping. My travel through the province also provided opportunities to collect data on the distribution and size of nesting colonies and diet of California and Ring-billed Gulls. That information expanded the database for my PhD thesis on those two species.

In the fall, I conducted aerial surveys of Trumpeter Swans in the Peace River. Those surveys helped determine the overall reproductive success of swans each year. It was exciting to see the majestic swans with their broods of cygnets on lakes and ponds from the air. The only setback was that I had to empty my stomach on several occasions due to turbulent weather and tight turns.

In December 1966, I was in charge of a CWS program to control the number of overwintering ducks in the Bow River near the Calgary airport. It was a conflict situation, as an association called "Friends of the Ducks" fed the ducks regularly, which led to an increase of the duck population. However, the airport manager wanted to reduce the number of ducks, as they constituted a danger to aircraft. To reduce the duck population, I asked the Royal Canadian Mounted Police (RCMP) to assist me. The RCMP agreed, and a dozen officers volunteered to shoot the ducks. Besides the RCMP, half a dozen CWS staff participated. Several hundreds of ducks were donated to the Salvation Army to mitigate any political ramifications which one could expect from such a program. My action proved to be prudent, as later, a non-government organization accused CWS staff of taking the ducks home for personal consumption.

In the summer of 1967, I began a survey of nesting colonies of Double-crested Cormorants, American White Pelicans, and Great Blue Herons in Alberta, as little was known then about their ecology and population status in that province. Cormorants and pelicans were surveyed at the same time, as they often nest on the same islands. Herons were surveyed separately, as they nest mostly in trees near water.

After discovering that colonies disappeared because of ongoing vandalism and destruction by humans, the objectives of my investigation changed. I extended the surveys of colonies into Saskatchewan and Manitoba, until the census was complete in the three Prairie provinces. The reason for the extension was to establish a solid foundation of the population status of cormorants, pelicans, and herons in the Prairie provinces, which would serve as a basis for measuring future population changes. Another important goal of the investigation now became to inform the Canadian public on the status of endangered colonies and to urge for their protection where necessary.

This story is based on reports which are cited in the next sections. They were submitted to journals such as *Blue Jay* and *Canadian Field-Naturalist* soon after the surveys were completed in order that either federal or provincial authorities could use the information to protect endangered colonies if they wished to do so.

Cormorants and Pelicans in Alberta and Saskatchewan

Cormorant and pelican colonies in Alberta were surveyed by car and boat, but also by plane at less accessible places in the province.[1] Only three small cormorant and four pelican colonies were found. Five cormorant and eight pelican colonies had disappeared by the time of my census. Several of the extinct cormorant and pelican colonies disappeared as a result of human disturbance.[2,3] Soper urged sanctuary protection for a pelican colony at Newell reservoir.[3] No such protection was given, and the nesting population of pelicans dwindled from 157 to 27 nests in 1966. No nesting pelicans were observed at Newell reservoir during my survey in 1967.

The next survey was conducted in Saskatchewan in 1968.[4] Nine cormorant and eight pelican colonies with 1,078 and 6,558 nests were counted, respectively. A pelican colony with 2,256 nests on Backes Island at Primrose Lake proved to be the largest in Canada at that time. Interestingly, Primrose Lake was also within the Canada Air Weapons Range. Eight cormorant and five pelican colonies at ten lakes had disappeared by the time of my survey. Carson found an American White Pelican colony at Suggi Lake completely destroyed by fishers in 1964.[5] He then reported his findings to an official of the Saskatchewan Department of Natural Resources. Carson reported that the official condemned the pelicans as a serious menace to the fishing industry and that no sanction would be given to the birds. Houston described his visits to the American White Pelican colony at Doré Lake as follows: "The conservation officer informed me that local ranchers were in the habit of taking boatloads of eggs from these colonies to feed their mink, rationalizing that the fish-eating birds were harmful to the fishing interests on the lake."[6]

Completion of American White Pelican Census in Canada

In 1969, colonies of American White Pelicans in Manitoba were surveyed by float plane as many were situated on isolated islands of large lakes.[7] The Manitoba census, together with a pelican colony investigated at Stum Lake in British Columbia in 1968, and at another one at Lake of the Woods in Ontario in 1969, completed my census of nesting American White Pelicans in Canada. On the basis of a count of 14,103 nests, the total breeding population in Canada was estimated at 30,000 birds for the years 1967–69, seven times higher than previous estimates.[7] I felt happy for having documented the nesting population of American White Pelicans in Canada, which future census conductors can use for comparison. It was the first serious effort to count the nesting population of American White Pelicans in Canada. Previous estimates were based on reviews of related literature and correspondence with naturalists and ornithologists.

After completing the census, I gained insight into some aspects of the ecology of American White Pelicans, in other words, the interaction between those birds and their environment. It appeared that the breeding range boundaries of American White Pelicans in Canada are chiefly determined by the general availability of fish as controlled by climatic and geological conditions.[7] Factors affecting nesting pelicans within their breeding range are human disturbance, fluctuating lake levels and mammalian predation. Houston reported that several pelican colonies disappeared as a result of falling lake levels in Saskatchewan.[6] Blokpoel reported that a family of foxes caused the failure of pelicans to raise any young in 1970 on Backes Island.[8] Backes Island in Primrose Lake contained the largest colony of American White Pelicans in Canada in 1968.[4]

Cormorants in Manitoba—Status at Lake Winnipegosis After Destruction

A total of 4,772 nests in 37 active colonies of Double-crested Cormorants were counted in Manitoba in 1969.[9] The largest nesting concentration of cormorants was found at Lake Winnipegosis, with 1,403 nests in 12 colonies. The Lake Winnipegosis census was important, as Mcleod and Bondar had launched a massive control program of cormorants there during the 1940s and early 1950s.[10] Thousands of eggs and nestlings had been destroyed, even though the cormorant diet was composed of only 7.2 percent commercial fish. Independent of that program, fishers and loggers also contributed to the destruction of cormorants.

There were thirty-six thousand cormorants on just four of the seventeen nesting reefs at Lake Winnipegosis at the start of the control program, but only 4,656 nests were counted immediately after its termination in 1951.[10] Eighteen years later, I observed that the cormorant population had dwindled to 1,403 nests, perhaps as a result of further destruction.

Protection for Cormorant and Pelican Colonies

Fortunately, there is an upside to the story. In articles and notes, I persisted with my calls for protection of cormorant and pelican colonies in the Prairie provinces.[1,4,11,12,13] It was not until my 1971 publication in the *Canadian Audubon* "The Pelican—protection or extinction," that five colonies were given protection. I concluded that article as follows: "Many islands on which White Pelicans have located their colonies belong to the provincial government, and special protection for these would require little money. If the pelican colonies are not protected immediately, so that fishers and boaters are compelled to leave the birds undisturbed during their nesting period, man will soon be unable to enjoy the sight of White Pelicans soaring majestically against blue prairie skies." Between 1976 and 1983, both cormorants and pelicans had dramatically increased in number.[14]

American White Pelicans on reef in Lake Winnipegosis, Manitoba, 1969.

Great Blue Herons in the Prairie Provinces

Nesting colonies of Great Blue Herons in Alberta were surveyed in 1967 as part of a CWS program to protect threatened birds.[15] Most heronries were located by asking biologists, wardens, and naturalists if they knew of colonies in their areas. Others were found by searching apparently suitable habitats along rivers and around lakes. A heronry with eleven active nests, in low willow bushes on an island in Dowling Lake, was studied in detail in 1968 because of its accessibility.

Most heronries were located in the southern half of the province. A total of twenty-seven colonies were found, ranging in size from a few to fifty-five nests. Eight colonies had been reported to be extinct at the time of my survey, mostly because of vandalism or trees being cut down in heronries. Vandalism continued unabated at some active colonies. One naturalist informed me that twelve herons were shot at one colony, resulting in a decline from ten active nests in 1965 to only one nest in 1967. Another naturalist reported that fifteen herons were shot in another heronry. The Dowling Lake heronry disappeared in 1969 because of human disturbance. The herons at that lake may have moved three miles from there to trees along an adjacent pond, where they were not observed before. One heronry likely relocated because of a pair of Bald Eagles had begun nesting there.

Heronries in Saskatchewan were surveyed in 1970 and in Manitoba in 1969 and 1971.[16,17,18] A total of 123 active heronries with 3,764 nests were found in the three Prairie provinces during the 1969–71 survey.[19] Based on that figure, it was estimated that the total breeding population of Great Blue Herons in those provinces consisted of at least four thousand breeding pairs. All heronries were located near water, and almost half were on lake islands. All but two of the 123 colonies were observed in trees. Two small colonies were located on treeless islands where herons nested directly on the ground in association with American White Pelicans, Double-crested Cormorants, Herring and Ring-billed Gulls, and Caspian and Common Terns. The largest heronries were found in the Lake Manitoba-Lake Winnipegosis region. The size of the sixteen colonies in that area averaged seventy nests.

Immigrant Gone to Heaven

Ground nest of Great Blue Herons at Talbot Lake, Manitoba, 1969.

Aquatic Park Proposal for Lake Winnipegosis

Besides herons, the largest concentration of cormorant and pelican colonies were found in the Lake Manitoba-Lake Winnipegosis region. The concentration of fish-eating birds there was thought to relate to an abundant supply of fish in those lakes.[19] The existence of a rich aquatic bird fauna was the main reason I recommended that Lake Winnipegosis and at least part of Kawinaw Lake and Pelican Lake should be set aside as a federal or provincial park for the birds' protection in an article in *Blue Jay*.[12]

One reason that the recommendation did not go anywhere is that I failed to go through the proper channels. Perhaps Nature Saskatchewan can "take up the torch from my failing hands" and nominate Lake Winnepegosis as a World Heritage Site, since Manitoba does not have a single established or listed site in Canada's Tentative List of World Heritage sites. Parks Canada is the lead agency for implementing the

World Heritage Convention, and manages the process for Canada. If Lake Winnipegosis becomes a World Heritage site, Canada would be the proud owner of the largest wild freshwater park in central North America.

Meeting Stuart Houston

My CWS supervisor took me to hunt Canada Geese in southern Alberta. After I had shot my first goose and felt sorry for the dead bird, I knew I was not a hunter. Most CWS managers and biologists were then both bird and big game hunters. I wanted more contact with naturalists for whom hunting was not their main hobby. One naturalist I met was Stuart Houston, a Saskatoon physician. Stuart invited me for a weekend of birding in the Saskatoon area. Banding of birds was Stuart's passionate hobby. In an article in *Blue Jay* entitled "R. F. Oldaker, the man who reads gull bands with a telescope," he estimated that he had banded "twenty-thousand-odd birds."[20] I knew Frank Oldaker, the subject of Stuart's article, very well from my study of Glaucous-winged Gulls on Mandarte Island in British Columbia. Frank contributed significantly to that study by reading band numbers of gulls I had banded and colour-coded at Mandarte in 1961 and 1962. Frank also produced valuable results for Stuart's large-scale project of banding California Gulls in Saskatchewan. A substantial number of Stuart's banded gulls were seen later on by Frank with his telescope in Vancouver.[20]

Stuart, his wife, and I had a great time birding, particularly at Redberry Lake where the highlight was a visit to the American White Pelican colony. I also assisted with the banding of a number of nestling pelicans at that lake. It felt like some kind of resource partitioning between two kindred spirits. I documented the status of colonial fish-eating birds and Stuart banded them. Stuart and I kept contact after our first meeting.

Pursuing the Trail of Pesticides and Mercury in Aquatic Birds

As with many stories, one thing leads to another. In 1968, I was transferred from the CWS Migratory Birds Section to the Pesticide Section because of my work on fish-eating birds, which were suspected to contain high levels of DDE residue. Although the CWS Pesticide Section was small, it strongly influenced how CWS evolved. I contributed by producing publications on organochlorine and mercury residues found in aquatic birds throughout the Prairie Provinces. These publications reveal which species were most at risk from pollutants, and where the birds were located. One investigation, entitled "Spotted Sandpipers as possible indicators of mercury contamination in rivers," published in *Blue Jay*,[1] combined with the discovery of my neighbour having a freezer full of mercury-contaminated fish caught in the North Saskatchewan River downstream of Edmonton, led to the discovery that industry and the University in Edmonton were sources of mercury pollution. The revelation of those sources made news in the Edmonton Journal to the chagrin of the CWS director at that time, who accused me of exposing "good corporate citizens of Edmonton."

Little was known about the extent of pesticide residues present in aquatic birds in Alberta, Saskatchewan, and Manitoba, so I began a massive sampling program of eggs from sixteen aquatic bird species at thirty-one locations in those provinces.[2] Eggs were chosen to be analyzed, as they are easy to collect and constitute distinct units of comparison. One significant result of that program was that high levels of DDE were discovered in Great Blue Heron eggs from Alberta.[2,3] Shell thickness was found to be significantly and inversely correlated with the concentration of DDE in those eggs. Besides fish-eating birds, reduced shell thickness has been found to be correlated with the amount of DDE in the egg contents of raptors.[4,5] Experimental studies with Mallards had shown that DDE can reduce thickness and cracking of eggshells.[6]

When a visiting Scandinavian student found elevated levels of mercury residues in some Canadian birds, I immediately had the same set of bird egg samples analyzed for mercury residues. I presented the information on mercury residue levels in aquatic birds in the Canadian Prairie Provinces to the North American Wildlife and Nature Resources Conference in 1971.[7] Each seat in the auditorium was taken, as mercury contamination was a new and hot topic at the time. At the end of the presentation, a lively discussion ensued. We discussed the differences in uptake of mercury by seed-eating and fish-eating birds. Seed-eating birds obtained alkyl mercury compounds from feeding on mercury-treated grain and seeds, while birds feeding on fish and aquatic invertebrates acquire inorganic mercury or phenyl mercury compounds in the form of slimicides released by chlor-alkali plants and pulp mills. Mercury levels in fish-eating birds were observed to be much higher than those in seed-eating birds. Several questions were from people who had just initiated an investigation of mercury residues in birds. For example, a biologist from Saskatchewan, who had begun an investigation of mercury in muscle tissues of Ring-necked Pheasants, Gray Partridge, and Sharp-tailed Grouse in the southern part of that province wanted to know about the relationship between mercury levels in eggs and muscles of those birds. He found that the levels of mercury in muscle tissue only in one case exceeded 0.05 parts per million. A biologist from Alaska who had started a mercury analysis program on fish in that state, asked if I had done any analysis on fish tissues, and if so, how did mercury residues stack up in fish that these birds consumed. I had not conducted such analysis, but because of my involvement in a study with the Freshwater Institute in Winnipeg, I learned that levels in fish were generally higher than in fish-eating birds. Discussions on other topics are documented in my presentation at that conference.[7]

Besides using large sampling programs of aquatic bird eggs, I examined bird tissues and aquatic invertebrates to determine whether they could serve as indicators of mercury contamination. One investigation, in which I examined the relationship between mercury in breast muscles and wing muscles of ducks, had immediate consequences. Annually, CWS collected tens of thousands of duck wings from hunters across Canada in order to determine the species, age, and sex composition of harvested birds. Muscle tissues adhering to the wings were analyzed to monitor levels of mercury in ducks. From a public perspective, it was important to know the mercury content in the muscle tissues used for human consumption. If the ratio of mercury residues in wing muscle to those in breast muscle were known, and if it did not vary significantly, such information would be useful in predicting levels of mercury in breast muscle. Fish in Clay Lake, which is part of the Wabigoon River system downstream of Dryden in western Ontario, were known to be among the most heavily contaminated by mercury in Canada. Therefore, five species of ducks were collected from that location prior to the hunting season. Highly significant correlations were found between levels of mercury in breast and wing muscles of Blue-winged Teals, Mallards, Common Goldeneyes, and Common Mergansers.[8] In spite of the small sample size (seven birds) of Hooded Mergansers, there still was a significant correlation between mercury levels in breast and wing muscles. As a result of the high levels of mercury found in the ducks' breast muscles, the hunting season was closed for all ducks in that region.

Breast muscles of Hooded Mergansers at Clay Lake contained the highest levels of mercury.[8,9] Hooded Mergansers fed on crayfish, which of all food items were most contaminated with mercury.[9] Consequently, I examined whether the crayfish *Orconectes virilis*, which feeds on detritus and scavenges on fish, could serve as an indicator of mercury contamination. *Orconectes virilis* is also more restricted in its movements than fish and is the most widely distributed crayfish species in Canada. Crayfish were sampled at locations that were known to represent a range from low (Lake Winnipegosis) to very high (Clay Lake) mercury levels reported in fish. Mercury levels between crayfish from

Clay Lake, the Saskatchewan River, and Lake Winnipegosis varied significantly.[10] By contrast, mercury levels in crayfish sampled at eight different sampling stations from Clay Lake varied little.[10] I concluded that *Orconectes virilis* is a good indicator of mercury in different water bodies, provided the crayfish are within the same range of body weight. At low levels of contamination, crayfish muscle was a more reliable indicator of mercury than the whole animal. This was not surprising, as crayfish muscle contained three times as much mercury as the rest of its body. Besides crayfish at Clay Lake, mayfly nymphs, water scorpions, and water boatmen were also highly contaminated with mercury, which may reflect their predatory feeding habits on small aquatic animals.

Pesticide Effects on Birds in Rice Fields of Suriname, South America

Because of my work with contaminants in aquatic birds in Canada, the Director of the Surinam Lands Bosbeheer invited me to investigate the effects of pesticides on birds in the rice polders of Wageningen in Suriname in 1971. My friend, Arie Spaans, a Dutch ornithologist, who lived in Paramaribo at that time, was the catalyst for that request. In early October, I travelled from Edmonton to Paramaribo, the capital of Suriname. At that time, Paramaribo was an interesting white city with a Dutch colonial character. I initially stayed with Arie and his wife, and had a great time admiring tropical flowers, birds, and butterflies, as it was my first time in the tropics. Small green frogs lived in homes and were considered part of the household. Large beetles and beautiful butterflies entered the house at night through open windows, drawn in by the light.

After acquiring a Volkswagen, I moved on to Wageningen along the coast in the western part of the country, where I took up accommodation in Hotel De Wereld for the next two months. From there I conducted my research on the effects of pesticides on Snail Kites, egrets, and other birds on the eight-thousand-hectare rice growing project of the Stichting of Machinale Landbouw (SML).

Immigrant Gone to Heaven

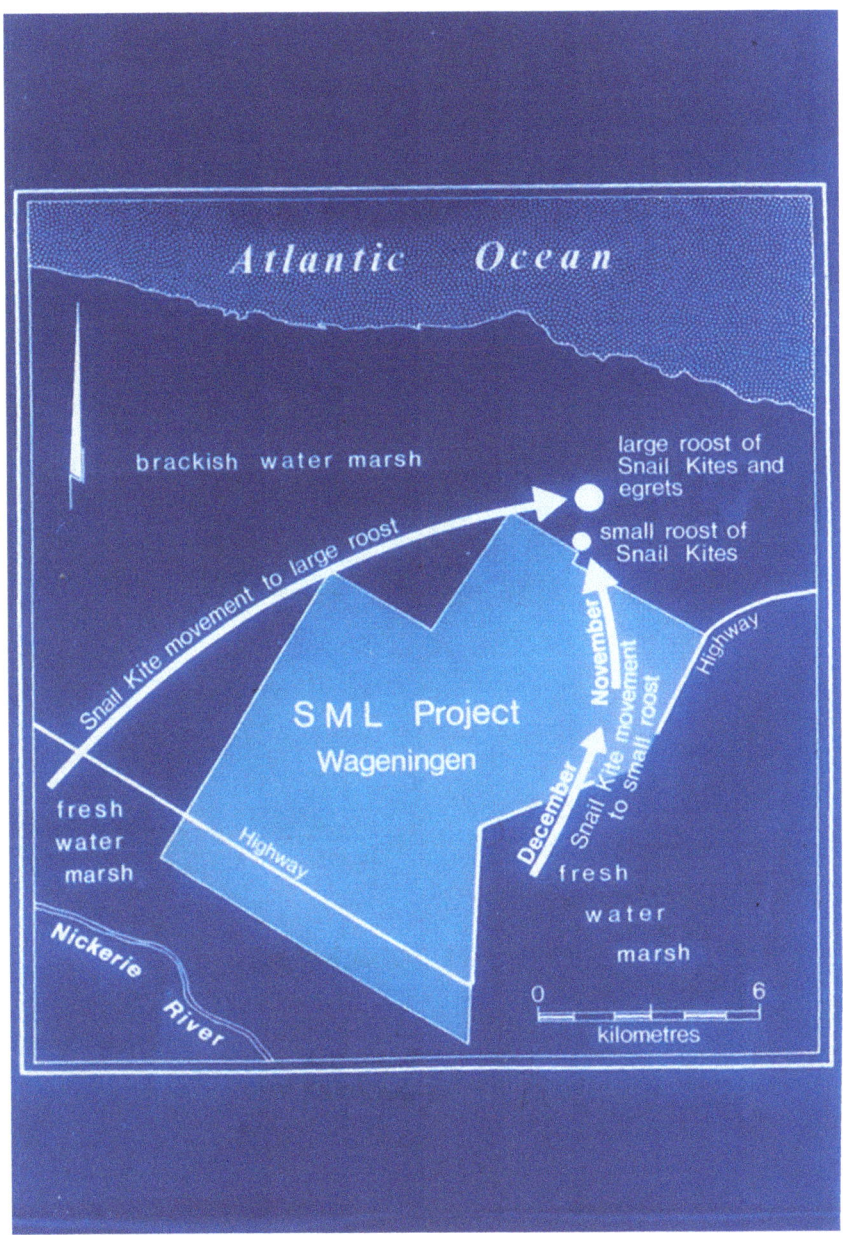

SML project in Suriname, South America.

Black Vultures on access road through SML rice paddies.

Local volunteer throws net to catch fishes in SML ditch.
Fishes, which Common and Snowy Egrets feed on,
were analyzed for pesticide residues.

Immigrant Gone to Heaven

Not unlike a detective, I loved piecing together the effects of sodium pentachlorophenate (NaPCP), the molluscicide sprayed by airplane to kill *Pomacea* snails feeding on rice plants in the polders. Thousands of fishes were also killed in the rice paddies during the application of NaPCP. Many dead Snail Kites were found on their roosts in the brackish water marsh north of the polders, as a result of eating the NaPCP-contaminated snails in the adjacent rice fields. Snail Kite organs were removed for pesticide analyses and the cadavers thrown afterwards into a polder ditch, where they were devoured within a few minutes by piranhas. Our study was one of the first well documented studies of the effects of NaPCP on birds of prey in an aquatic habitat.[11] Because of the observed mass mortality of Snail Kites resulting from the application of NaPCP in the rice fields, we recommended that another, less toxic pesticide with a shorter half-life should be used to control *Pomacea* snails. That recommendation was followed up and Snail Kite mortality decreased dramatically. Besides NaPCP, the effects of other pesticides (such as Endrin) on birds were investigated as well. At the end of the study, I presented in Dutch my preliminary findings to SML staff and other interested parties. A journalist from the main Paramaribo newspaper was present at the meeting. Shortly afterward, the story was major news.

Disposal of NaPCP barrels.
SML staff were advised to dispose of the barrels safely, as commercial preparations of NaPCP contain high levels of dioxin, a known teratogenic (malformations and monstrosities) compound.

Fishes killed in rice paddy after spraying of NaPCP.
Chemical analysis showed high levels of pentachlorophenol
in pooled samples of dead fishes.

Kees Vermeer searching for dead birds (Snail Kites and Egrets) in brackish water marsh adjacent to SML rice polder.

Dead Snail Kite beneath a black mangrove bush in brackish water marsh.

Several species of herons and egrets (eight), caracaras, hawks, kites, and vultures (ten), and plovers, sandpipers, and yellowlegs (seven), as well as other birds associated with aquatic habitats such as gallinules, limpkins, jacanas, and terns were observed in the rice polders and adjacent brackish water marsh.[11] All seven species of shorebirds that I observed were North American migrants, of which Upland Plovers, Spotted Sandpipers, and Greater and Lesser Yellowlegs are widely distributed nesting birds in the Canadian Prairie Provinces.[12] North America and coastal Suriname share tens of thousands of shorebirds, and at least sixteen species, of which the Semipalmated Sandpiper is the most numerous migrant from Alaska and Canada.[13]

Besides my field research, Arie and I made a boat trip along the Coppename River from Bitagron to the Voltzberg-Raleigh Falls Nature Reserve in the interior of Suriname. Along the river there were small settlements where women prepared manioc, and beautiful coloured macaws flew from treetop to treetop. When we arrived at the falls, a magnificent Harpy Eagle watched us. At night, we slept in hammocks beneath the roof of an open building. I woke up frequently, because Arie had told me to watch for vampire bats, which might suck my blood through the hammock. In the morning, we were greeted by the loud calls of howler monkeys that sounded like distant thunder. In rock pools near the falls, I watched with fascination giant electric eels moving around. We explored the area of the dome-shaped Voltzberg with its interesting flora growing in cirques on smooth granite flats. Unfortunately, I did not see the bright orange Guianan Cock-of-the-Rock, which was known to occur near the Voltzberg.

After our camping trip to the Voltzberg-Raleigh Falls Nature Reserve, Arie took me to a marsh near Paramaribo where there were supposed to be Scarlet Ibises. I had never seen one in the wild before, only birds with faded plumage in a zoo. Slugging through the marsh on a dark morning, I saw my first Scarlet Ibis. Its brilliant red plumage did not seem real; perhaps it was my imagination, but the ibis seemed to light up the dark morning sky.

Immigrant Gone to Heaven

Voltzberg in Suriname.

Back in Wageningen, I prepared and sorted my frozen samples of bird tissues, fishes, frogs, and snails for pesticide analyses in Canada. I planned to visit Ottawa first to drop off the frozen samples before going home to Edmonton. I needed to let the CWS staff in Ottawa know the exact time of my arrival so the samples would remain preserved and not spoil. In the meantime, an SML staff invited me for a boat ride on the Maratakka River near Wageningen, where we visited a village of native inhabitants. They were friendly, and one woman gave me a large bunch of cooking bananas. I bought a beautiful purple Phalaenopsis orchid growing from a coconut husk, which I later brought back with me to Edmonton. There it adorned our living room for months during the long cold winter.

When it was time to leave, I drove my Volkswagen with the samples to Paramaribo. From there I left by airplane for Ottawa, where I dropped my samples off at midnight to the dedicated CWS staff. The next morning, I arrived in Edmonton, just in time to spend Christmas at home with my wife and daughter. The investigation in Suriname taught me that toxic chemical problems can be readily solved by a small multidisciplinary team with the required expertise. The closer countries and organizations cooperate, the better for humankind and the environment.

Back to Seabirds in British Columbia

CWS Edmonton, 1972–75

In 1972, I was transferred from the Pesticide Section back to the Migratory Birds Section of the CWS. I had no choice in the transfer, and felt unhappy with my new and authoritarian supervisor. Although working conditions became difficult, I still produced significant work. One main objective was to conduct a review of the potential effects of oil spills on marine birds on the west coast of Canada. Rebecca, who had just finished her Master of Science program in Physical Chemistry in Edmonton, obtained a CWS contract to review the effects of oil spills on birds in the world's oceans. She conducted an extensive search of the literature, which resulted in two annotated bibliographies—one on the impact of oil on birds, and the other on aquatic organisms. Both were a first on the subject. Together, we produced a timely and significant review of the effects of oil spills on seabirds on the west coast of Canada, which was welcomed by researchers in the field (see Part IV—Alan Burger's Tribute). Partly because of that review, an opportunity arose for me to be transferred from CWS Edmonton to CWS Vancouver in British Columbia, from where I would conduct research on seabirds.

Move to Vancouver Island

We sold our house in Sherwood Park in May 1975. We were sorry to leave our home where we had shared many good memories. Rebecca and Lotus were sad to leave their friends behind. I felt relieved, because I no longer had to deal with constrained working conditions. Our belongings were transported by a huge moving van to our new home on Mainwaring Road in North Saanich, Vancouver Island. Even our houseplants, picnic table, and garbage cans were shipped, as moving costs were covered by CWS. The van was scheduled to arrive on Mainwaring Road on June 4. In the meantime, we left our home in Sherwood Park on May 30. Lotus's little dog, Maya, travelled with us. We stayed overnight with Filipino friends in Fort Saskatchewan, and the next morning, we drove to BC. I was happy to be back in that province. We stayed overnight in Golden and Hope, and on June 2 we arrived in Sidney on Vancouver Island, where we booked into a motel. On the morning of June 4, the van with our belongings arrived as scheduled. It took the crew only a few hours to unload the furniture. By noon we were enjoying lunch in our new home on Mainwaring Road, where we still live today.

Lotus (with dog) and friends at Sherwood Park, Alberta, 1974.

Although my new CWS office was on the BC mainland, Rebecca and I chose to live near Sidney because of its rural atmosphere and my good memories of that town when I studied Glaucous-winged Gulls on Mandarte Island in 1961–62. That meant I had to commute by ferry each weekday to my office on the mainland. After two years, I was given an office at the Institute of Ocean Sciences in North Saanich. That saved many hours of commuting to and from the mainland.

I prepared for my research on seabirds, and chose Triangle Island for my first field project because it had the largest seabird colonies in the province. Triangle Island is a small, isolated, and uninhabited island at the northwestern tip of Vancouver Island.

Preparation for Fieldwork

The cheapest and quickest way to travel to Triangle Island was by helicopter from Port Hardy, a town in northern Vancouver Island. I hired an assistant called Dan. By mid-June, we loaded provisions in my government vehicle, including a prefabricated toolshed, which we planned to use for living and sleeping quarters. We drove to Port Hardy, parked the vehicle at the airport, and loaded the provisions and the toolshed in a net, which was slung beneath the helicopter. On Triangle Island, we assembled the toolshed at the edge of a sheltered bay on a flat area just above the southern shore. The location appeared to be a previous dwelling site used by North American natives. We discovered artifacts and extensive midden beds of mussels intermixed with bird, mammal and fish bone remains and clam shells. We built an outhouse and a table from driftwood found along the shore, and acquired our drinking water from a little creek on a nearby slope. We found this little creek with the help of the gulls, which were drinking from pools on the beach below the creek.

Field camp on Triangle Island, BC, 1975.

Family Time on Triangle Island

Toward the end of the seabirds' nesting season, I relieved my assistant on Triangle Island. Instead, I brought along Rebecca and Lotus, who enjoyed the island immensely. They would go beachcombing for glass ball floats. We took out our inflatable rubber boat and fished for rockfish, which were plentiful and easy to catch near shore. Rebecca collected sea snails at low tide, which she cooked in the shell. We had great fun twirling the snail meat out of the shell with a safety pin—a novel way for me to eat the snails.

At night, we gazed at the beautiful, star-spangled sky with no interference from urban lights. When we got into our sleeping bags on cots resting on boxes of groceries in our small toolshed, large deer mice jumped on us from the clothes hanging on the wall of the shed. We called them super mice, and counted the snapping of the traps, which we had set up for them, until we fell asleep. Sometimes we would be awakened at night by a stream of oats, flour, or sugar on our faces when the mice chewed holes into the storage bags on the shelves above us. We did not catch all the mice. On some mornings, we found they had built nests in my socks. The nests made my toes curl into uneasy surprise when I put on my socks.

Rebecca, Lotus, and Kristine waiting for helicopter on Triangle Island, 1975.

Rabbits

One day, Kristine, a school friend Lotus had brought along to Triangle Island, caught a rabbit. Rabbits were common on the island and were the offspring of European rabbits introduced by a lightkeeper in the 1920s when, for a brief period, there was a lighthouse on the island. Lotus wanted a rabbit also, but did not catch one. Back home we bought her a Dutch rabbit, which we kept in a cage. Lotus and her friend played with their rabbits together. One day, to our surprise, Lotus's rabbit produced a litter. Lotus gave berry names to the rabbits such as Raspberry, Blueberry, Blackberry, and Gooseberry. After a while, I ended up looking after the rabbits when I came home from my office on the mainland late at night. When the rabbits became too much of a burden, I contacted Mr. Cook, a neighbour. We met late one evening and shook hands for the first time. Mr. Cook, in a melodramatic voice, said, "It is too bad we have to meet under such tragic circumstances." I did not know how tragic matters would become.

Soon after, our little dog Maya came home with a rabbit head, which it had picked up from Mr. Cook's compost heap. When Lotus saw the head, she cried out "It is Raspberry!" She buried the rabbit head in the garden with a little ceremony in a grave she marked with the name, Raspberry. The following day, Maya dug up the grave and Lotus and Rebecca had to go through the painful ceremony again. A few days later, Maya came back with another rabbit head. Lotus cried out "It is Blackberry!" We can laugh at it now, but at that time, I was afraid to hear more rabbit tales when I returned home from work.

Lotus and Rebecca's Adaptation

Lotus missed her close friend Nadia and others from Sherwood Park. Although a family with children of Lotus's age lived next to us, she did not always feel welcome because of sibling rivalry within that family. It also took her time to adjust to her new school. Lotus's situation changed much for the better a few years later, when she took up horse riding. She developed a strong bond with her first horse, a pony called Thistledown. Through her love of horses, she met other girls who had taken up the hobby of horse riding. They became her friends. Her friendship with Elizabeth, her riding companion, has lasted to the present day.

Rebecca adjusted easily to our new home environment. She attended the University of Victoria during our first summer in BC. Her advisor told her she would do well to take up economics as a profession. She followed his advice and enrolled in an Honours Program in Economics that fall. After completing her program with distinction in two years, she enrolled in an MA program, which she completed in one year. By that time, Rebecca had two Master degrees—one in Chemistry and the other in Economics. Thereafter, she was employed as a government economist in various ministries such as Finance, Energy, Mines & Petroleum Resources, and Health.

Seabird Studies and Tragedy on Triangle Island

I began my first field studies on Triangle Island because BC's largest seabird colonies are found there. I did not know how large until I surveyed them. No serious research had been previously done on seabirds there, perhaps because it is a remote and uninhabited island in the Scott Island Archipelago, forty-six kilometres offshore the northwestern tip of Vancouver Island.[1] Even today, Triangle Island is, in my mind, the most fabulous place for studying seabirds on Canada's west coast. As its name implies, the island is roughly triangular in shape. Its highest point, 210 metres above sea level, was the site of an active light station from 1909 to 1919. Now only the concrete shell of the lighthouse and foundations of dwellings remain. The island rises steeply on all sides from the Pacific Ocean. Large boulders and logs are strewn over its beaches. Frequent rain and fog occur. The latter gives it a misty atmosphere. Most of the island is covered by salmon berries, which are pruned by strong winds. Trees are absent. Tufted hair grass covers the hill slopes extensively, and appears to be the preferred nesting habitat for Rhinoceros Auklets and Tufted Puffins.

Triangle Island as seen from the air.

Campsite on Triangle Island in 1976.

Immigrant Gone to Heaven

Puffin Rock—best known landmark of Triangle Island.

**Tufted Puffins near nesting burrows on Puffin Rock.
(Photo Credit: Canadian Wildlife Service)**

In March 1976, I was fortunate to obtain the use of an abandoned trailer located at the island summit, previously used by Shell Oil for offshore exploration. As the trailer was of little use to us where it was located, I asked Shell Oil for permission to use the trailer and relocate it. Shell Oil was happy to get rid of the trailer, as Triangle Island had become part of an Ecological Reserve. I had the trailer hooked up to a cargo helicopter and moved to our campsite near the beach. Now our accommodation was much more comfortable, and the toolshed became a storage shed.

Surveys of Nesting Populations

At least twelve species of seabirds nest on Triangle Island, of which Tufted Puffins, Rhinoceros Auklets, and Cassin's Auklets were most numerous. All three species nest in burrows dug into the soil, where they lay their eggs and raise their young. We set out quadrats at predetermined intervals along transect lines in different types of vegetation and at various elevations and slope angles to determine the size of the nesting populations.

Surveys in 1975 and 1976 determined that there were approximately fifteen thousand nesting pairs of Tufted Puffins and twenty-five thousand pairs of Rhinoceros Auklets.[2] Cassin's Auklets were by far the most numerous. Our extensive survey in 1977 showed that there were approximately 360,000 nesting pairs of Cassin's Auklets on Triangle Island.[3] It was a thrill to discover that Triangle Island contained the largest nesting colony for that species in the world! Even larger numbers were observed on Triangle Island when it was resurveyed in 1989. It was then estimated there were 550,000 nesting pairs of Cassin's Auklets on Triangle Island, with a total of nearly one million pairs in the Scott Island Archipelago as a whole.[4] Our investigations at Triangle Island in 1975–77 and at Frederick and Langara Islands in Haida Gwaii in 1980–81, laid the foundation for documenting BC's populations of burrow-nesting alcids.[5] Two of my assistants, Moira Lemon and Michael Rodway, continued the inventory of burrow-nesting seabirds in BC. CWS should continue these inventories for key areas on a regular basis. Only then can the effects of environmental perturbations on BC's nesting seabird populations be accurately measured.

Research on Rhinoceros Auklets and Tufted Puffins

Rhinoceros Auklets and Tufted Puffins are closely related species, and feed on the same type of fishes, which they bring crosswise in their bills to their nestlings. Tufted Puffins feed their nestlings during the day, while Rhinoceros Auklets do so at night. Seasonal changes in prey fish populations can affect the birds' reproductive success. For example, on Triangle Island, Rhinoceros Auklets raised their young successfully when the nestling diet changed from small sand lances and rockfishes in July, to larger Pacific sauries in August.[6,7] However in 1976, the auklets' reproductive success was poor and chick growth slow when sauries dominated the birds' diet in July.[7] A large number of chicks then died, showing symptoms of starvation and weakness. Many sauries brought to the chicks in 1976 were found in the burrows uneaten. Saury tails protruded from mouths of small live chicks. Dead chicks were seen with a saury protruding from their bill, indicating the chicks had choked on the saury. Yet, when similar-size sauries were fed to advanced chicks in August, the nestlings thrived, as was evident by their healthy weights. The timing of the appearance of sauries in the auklets' breeding cycle is therefore critical to the survival of nestlings.[7]

Rhinoceros Auklet.
(Photo Credit: AdobeStock 142 947401)

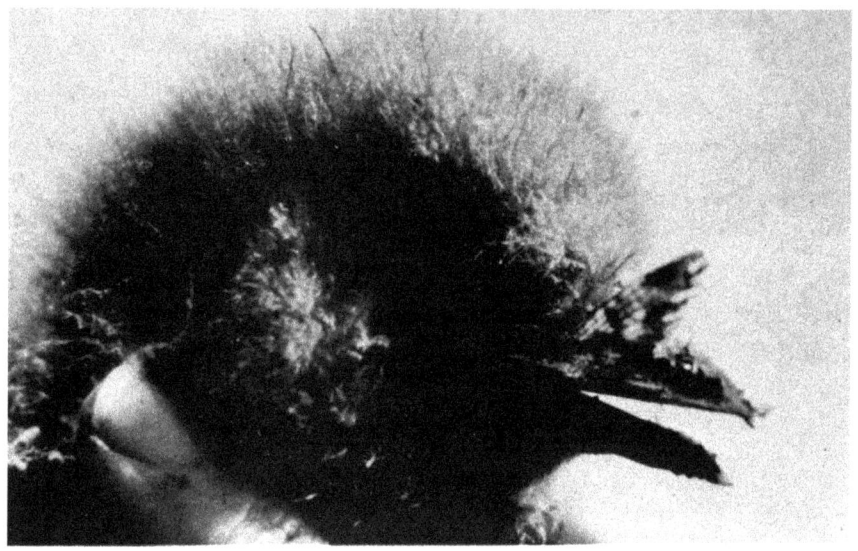

Rhinoceros Auklet chick (alive) with saury tail protruding from mouth. (Photo Credit: The Canadian Wildlife Service)

Annual changes in prey availability can also affect the reproductive success of seabirds. For example, in five years of study, Tufted Puffins failed extensively to raise young in three years, reproduced moderately in one year, and did well in another.[2] The extensive failure in three years may have been due to adverse weather conditions and unavailability of sand lances, a major food source for puffins.[8] In the most successful year (1978), puffins mainly fed on sand lances and bluethroat argentines, a coldwater and deep-sea species. The argentines' sudden and mass appearance in the diet of nestling puffins (as well as that of Rhinoceros Auklets) only in 1978 probably related to strong upwelling in the Triangle Island area and the nearby Vancouver Island coast.[2] Merv Campbell, a salmon fisher, also observed that salmon extensively fed on argentines in that area and year, which he and other fishers had not seen previously. In subsequent CWS studies on Triangle Island, no further mass appearance of argentines were observed in the diet of puffins and Rhinoceros Auklets.

Anne Vallée

In the summer of 1982, Anne Vallée, a PhD student from Quebec, conducted a study on Tufted Puffins on Triangle Island. She was in need of financial support to continue her studies and she asked me for help. I was able to obtain a CWS contract for her to keep her puffin research going. In return, Anne would assist the CWS staff with collecting census data on nesting puffins. We became friends and my thirteen-year-old daughter Lotus spent time with Anne and her assistant on Triangle Island. After Lotus' return from the Island, Moira Lemon, a CWS census technician spelled off Anne's assistant. Anne helped Moira with the CWS census of puffins. Both had radiotelephone contact with me. On July 31, Moira phoned me, and although the radio signal was poor, I could make out that something terrible had happened. Moira told me that she had been surveying puffin burrows with Anne on a steep slope on the north side of the island, when suddenly Anne had disappeared. She did not know where Anne had gone, as Anne followed at some distance behind her. After some searching, Moira looked over the edge of a cliff, and saw Anne's body lying at the shore. Moira tried to resuscitate Anne, but to no avail. After that, Moira slugged through the shrubbery across the island to the campsite, and called me on the field radio. Understandably, Moira was shaken.

I kept radio contact with Moira and notified the RCMP immediately. The RCMP could not reach Triangle Island by helicopter because of fog. Moira remained for several days on the island before the RCMP arrived, who picked up Moira and collected Anne's body. In the meantime, I had the difficult task of notifying Anne's parents of their daughter's death. Later, the Vallées, who knew that Anne had been a family friend, visited and spent a weekend with us. To honour and remember Anne, the British Columbia government renamed the Triangle Island Ecological Reserve the Anne Vallée Triangle Island Ecological Reserve in 1983.

One week after the tragedy, I attended a seabird symposium at King's College in Cambridge, England. A CWS seabird colleague from eastern Canada asked how my summer went. After I told him what had happened, he grew silent. He also had recently lost a technician in a boat accident near a seabird colony in Newfoundland. A Norwegian biologist who visited me for a week at my home told of similar casualties during seabird studies on sea cliffs in Norway. But whatever the risks, dedicated seabird biologists continue their frequently dangerous fieldwork on remote islands and sea cliffs in the world's seas and oceans.

Rhinoceros Auklet Fish Sampling Expeditions

From 1976 to 1980, I conducted research on the fish diet of Rhinoceros Auklet nestlings on islands along the British Columbia coast. The results of that study were published by the Canadian Wildlife Service.[1] The study showed that the Rhinoceros Auklet diet can be used for monitoring age classes of juvenile prey fish populations in surface waters. Here I will describe my experience with family members and others while conducting my research.

Rhinoceros Auklet in breeding plumage.
(Photo Credit: R. Wayne Campbell)

Jergen's Unforgettable Remarks

My co-author of the above-mentioned publication, the late Jergen Westerheim, was a retired research scientist studying fishes at the Pacific Biological Station in Nanaimo. Jergen was of Norwegian descent, of which he was proud. I often visited him at his home or office to consult with him about the identity of juvenile fishes, which was not always easy to establish, particularly for rockfishes. When I informed Jergen how beautiful some fishes looked when freshly caught from auklet beaks, he said, "Kees, you are so lucky to see them in their natural colours. At the station, we see them when they are in bottles with formaldehyde." At another time, he remarked, "Kees, we know very little about juvenile fish populations, but your auklet study shows things which ichthyologists can only dream about."

Islands Selected for Sampling

Three islands were selected for sampling fishes from Rhinoceros Auklets, as they contain large nesting populations of those birds. Pine and Triangle Islands are located near the northern tip of Vancouver Island, while Lucy Island is farther to the north, near Prince Rupert. Pine and Lucy Islands are forested, but Triangle Island is treeless. Both Pine and Lucy Islands have lightkeepers with established lighthouses. Triangle Island had a lighthouse in the past, but has none to date. On several occasions, Rebecca and Lotus accompanied me on sampling expeditions to Pine and Triangle Islands. Since my journey to Triangle Island with my wife and daughter has been described in chapter 5, I will relate here a memorable visit with my brother Jan, together with Rebecca and Lotus, to Pine Island.

Jan's Visit to Pine Island

Jan, who lived in the Netherlands, had been an ardent fisher all his life. During the years that the Netherlands was occupied during WWII, Jan's fishing in the Dutch polder contributed to much-needed protein on the table for our wanting family. In the summer of 1980, Jan visited Canada for a holiday. Since that was his first visit (and only one, as Jan passed away in the eighties), I decided to treat him to a fishing trip he would never forget.

To reach Pine Island, I chartered a helicopter from Port Hardy, the nearest town to the island. The island had a helicopter pad. There were three houses on the island, one for the senior lightkeeper and his family, another for his assistant, and a third one for guests. We lived in relative comfort in the guesthouse, which was close to the helicopter pad.

Rhinoceros Auklets return to the island at night to feed their young. They crash into the bushes beneath the spruce trees on the way to their nesting burrows. Both parents carry fishes in their beaks for their young. With our backs bent, Lotus and I would chase the birds amongst the bushes. We would shine the light from a flashlight on the auklets to freeze them in position, which enabled us to take the fishes from their beaks. We would not stay at the same spot for long, to prevent doing harm to the young auklets in the burrows. After I identified, measured, and weighed each fish in the morning, they were used as bait by Jan, Rebecca, and Lotus for catching rockfishes and greenlings. Those fishes were dwelling at various water depths along a steep, rocky cliff near the lighthouse station.

The various rockfish species came in a dazzling array of colours. The cliffside was excellent fish habitat, as almost every cast of our improvised fishing gear resulted in a catch. The fishing gear consisted of a sturdy branch with a hook at the end of a weed wacker line. A heavy metal nut tied to the thick nylon line served as a sinker to counter the strong current. It was a fisher's paradise! Not only that, freshly caught and cooked rockfish taste delicious!

We spent six days on the island, and Jan fished almost daily. He caught more fish than what everybody at the lighthouse station could eat. Fortunately, there was a refrigerator room at the station, where we could store the fish. When the lightkeeper saw all the fish, he asked me to tell Jan to stop fishing. I tactfully broke the news to Jan. He walked perhaps ten times around the island trails that day, but the next morning he informed me that he was becoming bored without the fishing. I suggested to Jan to go to the other side of the island where the fishing was not as good. I also asked him to throw the fish back into the sea after he caught them. Jan seemed reluctant to comply with that request, as he was more of a provider than a conservationist by nature. During World War II, Jan took great risks to help our Dutch family to survive (see Part III – Our Family Adapts to the German Occupation).

When the time came for us to leave Pine Island, I called the Canadian Coast Guard for a helicopter to take us back to Port Hardy. The Coast Guard informed me that a Sikorsky helicopter, which happened to be in the neighbourhood, would soon land on the island. When the Sikorsky landed with a thundering noise on the helicopter pad, Jan was almost knocked off his feet by the draft of its whirling blades. He threw his arms up in utter bewilderment as I had not informed him of what was coming to pick us up. I will never forget that sight of Jan. When we arrived back at home, Jan and I donated all the fish we brought from Pine Island to the Salvation Army in Victoria.

Lucy Island

When I first arrived by Coast Guard at Lucy Island, a man on shore reached out his hand to help me jump off the boat. I immediately handed him a bottle of Dutch apricot brandy, which he received with a grin. He informed me that he was by himself, as his family was then in Prince Rupert. Although he was a Jehovah's Witness, we shared some of the brandy. His name was Keith Nuttall, and he was then the only lightkeeper on the island. I learned later that he had one glass eye. We got along fine.

His wife Dorothy and their children joined us later. When Keith informed them of the reason for my visit, they were excited, and one of his young daughters enthusiastically assisted with sampling of fishes from auklets each night. Lotus joined me on later visits to Lucy Island to help with catching auklets. During the day, Lotus would build sandcastles with the keeper's children on the beautiful sandy beaches. On some occasions, Keith took me fishing with his small boat, but we only caught smelly rat fishes, which we threw back into the water.

I much enjoyed being with the Nuttalls. They were a close-knit family, and never talked to me about their religion. One night while sampling fishes from auklets, I twisted a leg muscle and could hardly walk. Days later, a floatplane picked me up and brought me to Prince Rupert harbour.

I leaned on the pilot's shoulder to get off the plane and onto the jetty, and from there to the closest street, all the while hopping along on one foot. A taxi took me to Prince Rupert airport, where I was provided with a wheelchair before boarding a plane. When I arrived home by ambulance, Rebecca looked aghast. Always interested in health matters, Rebecca examined my leg and discovered a huge lump on my thigh. After one hour of massage, the lump subsided, and I could walk again.

Cassin's Auklets as Monitors of Zooplankton and Climate Change

In the late seventies and early eighties, I investigated what type of prey Cassin's Auklets, which are small diving birds, feed their young at night after having spent the night at sea.[1,2] The auklets' diet was examined on Triangle Island and compared with that on Frederick Island in Haida Gwaii, 345 kilometres to the north of Triangle Island in British Columbia.[2] Triangle and Frederick Islands are located in two different ecosystems, with Triangle Island near the northern end of the California Current Ecosystem, and Frederick Island to the north in the Alaska Current Ecosystem.

Cassin's Auklet, the most numerous seabird on Triangle Island.
(Photo Credit: R. Wayne Campbell)

The presence of the copepod *Neocalanus cristatus* in the auklets' diet, the most important and a high in energy food eaten, is compared to its availability and abundance in coastal waters. The same comparison is made for euphausiids, the second most important auklet food. Another subject is the monitoring of seabirds for environmental perturbances affecting their populations along the North Pacific Rim.

Food Collection and Processing

Cassin's Auklets bring zooplankton and larval fishes to their nestlings in a neck pouch. Auklets are easily sampled when caught in a net upon returning to their colonies to feed their young in burrows dug into the soil. They arrive there after it has turned dark and they have spent the day at sea. Food from parents was obtained by gently massaging their neck pouches, so they would regurgitate food through a funnel into pre-weighed containers. Samples were weighed and preserved in jars with 10 percent formaldehyde. The formaldehyde was removed in the laboratory by thoroughly rinsing the sample with water.

Moira Galbraith, an expert in handling food samples and zooplankton identification at the Institute of Ocean Sciences in North Saanich, processed and weighed samples of different food categories on an electronic balance, so that the frequency and biomass of each category and species could be determined. Zooplankton species were also measured so that their size could be compared between islands and years. Without Moira's assistance, it would have been difficult to investigate the auklet diet.

Food of Nestlings

Cassin's Auklets chiefly feed their nestlings the copepod *Neocalanus cristatus*, euphausiids and small fishes on Frederick and Triangle Islands.[1] [2]Euphausiids consisted of three species: *Thyssanoessa spinifera*, *Thyssanoessa longipes,* and *Euphausia pacifica*. Fishes were mostly digested and rarely identifiable. Some that could be identified were Pacific sand lances and Irish lords. Hyperiid amphipods were frequently eaten, but contributed little substance to auklet meals. Scyphozoid medusa, squid, octopus, and gooseneck barnacles were encountered occasionally. The largest prey was the euphausiid *T. spinifera* (20.9–33.6 mm); and the smallest were the copepods *Neocalanus plumchrus* and *Calanus pacificus* (2.5–4.6 mm). These two small copepods may be taken by auklets, as they possess conspicuous oil sacks with high lipid content.[2]

Importance of *Neocalanus cristatus*

Three species of copepods, *N. cristatus*, *N. plumcrus*, and *Eucalanus bungii* constitute most of the zooplankton biomass in the epipelagic zone of the subarctic Pacific,[3] of which only *N. cristatus*, the largest copepod, is taken by auklets in large quantities.[1,2] *N. cristatus* copepods made up significantly more of the food biomass, and were observed to be significantly larger in auklet meals on Frederick than on Triangle Island.[2] The late John Fulton observed that *N. cristatus* was the most numerous in northern British Columbia waters,[2] which is consistent with the greater *N. cristatus* biomass observed in the auklet diet at Frederick than at Triangle Island. *N. cristatus* declines to the south of British Columbia and is either absent or exceedingly rare in California's coastal waters, which explains its absence as a food for auklets there.[2] Instead, auklets in California feed upon the euphausiids, *T. spinifera* and *E. pacifica*.[2] Therefore, the Cassin's Auklet can serve as an indicator species of the abundance and changes in the composition of plankton prey over its extensive latitudinal breeding range.[4]

Cassin's Auklets breeding in British Columbia grow heavier than those farther south.[4] Most of the known nesting population of Cassin's Auklets is found in a relatively small portion of their breeding range from Triangle to Forrester Island on the Alaska-British Columbia boundary.[5] The simultaneous occurrences of heavier nestlings and a larger Cassin's Auklet population suggest greater availability of the high energy copepod *N. cristatus* in northern areas than in those farther to the south.[4] It is amazing that an eight-millimetre-long copepod *N. cristatus* governs the distribution and numbers of nesting Cassin's Auklets. If Cassin's Auklets can be called the seabird jewels of British Columbia, then it appears that the crown which holds the auklets there is an army of small copepods. How long the crown will be there to hold the jewels is anybody's guess.

Euphausiids

T. spinifera, *T. longipes*, and *E. pacifica* were the main euphausiids observed in the auklet diet. *T. longipes* was fed upon significantly more at Frederick than on Triangle Island. By contrast, *T. spinifera* was significantly more eaten by auklets on Triangle than at Frederick Island.[2] Of all zooplankton, the abundance of euphausiids has been best documented in British Columbia waters.[6] Among seventeen euphausiid species known to occur there, nine are accessible to Cassin's Auklets. The others have been found only in net samples at depths greater than two hundred metres.[6] Among the nine available species, *T. spinifera*, *T. longipes*, and *E. pacifica* account for 90 percent of the euphausiid biomass observed in surface waters.[6] The presence of those species in the auklet diet suggests that the birds prey upon the most available and abundant euphausiids.

Seabirds as Monitors

Seabirds can be used to monitor environmental perturbances affecting the marine environment. Annual and seasonal changes in diet can be easily documented. Frequent seabird inventories in key areas provide information about whether populations are increasing, decreasing, or remain the same. Reproductive failure, starvation, and poor growth suggest staple foods are unavailable or scarce. Both plankton-feeding Cassin's Auklets and fish-feeding Rhinoceros Auklets can be sampled and monitored for those parameters. Tufted Puffins, which feed fishes to their nestlings during the day, are another species which may serve as monitors. They provide additional information about how diurnal foragers are affected by oceanic changes. However, sampling food from puffins has its drawbacks, as they are easily disturbed during the sampling process.

Besides collecting food from birds, one needs to conduct complementary net sampling to establish the relationship of prey in surface waters to those observed in the birds' diet. Joint efforts between plankton, fish, and seabird biologists will enhance our understanding of the distribution and structure of both zooplankton and juvenile fish populations and their availability to marine birds. Neither discipline in itself provides an understanding of the changes that occur in zooplankton and juvenile fish populations. In a 1992 article[7] entitled "The diet of birds as a tool for monitoring the biological environment," I proposed that:

> A coordinated and integrated international program, including a number of strategically located seabird colony monitoring stations, should be established, including the Farallon Islands off California, Triangle Island off British Columbia, Forrester Island off southeastern Alaska, Middleton Island in the Gulf of Alaska, Buldir Island in the Aleutians, Teuri Island off Japan, and as yet a to be designated island off Pacific Russia. This would provide marine bird biologists with a major tool to measure, as well as an early warning system to determine the effects of annual physical changes, El Niños, and global warming in the oceanic environment on seabird populations and their prey over a vast region of the North Pacific.

That proposal is still valid at present. I only would add Frederick to Triangle in the above listed monitoring stations, as seabird colonies on Triangle and Frederick Islands are located in different marine ecosystems and could be affected by different oceanic conditions. Present seabird biologists have taken my Cassin's Auklet studies further and relate aspects of auklet biology to climate variability. Climate variability may have been a factor during my studies of auklets and puffins on Triangle Island in the seventies. At that time, I was unable to explain the massive reproductive failure of puffins observed on the island. I suggested that the puffin failures could have been the result of oceanic conditions affecting the birds' food supply.[8] To my knowledge, there were no biologists investigating the effects of climate change on seabirds in the seventies.

Storm-petrels in Haida Gwaii

Storm-petrels in Haida Gwaii were investigated from June 8 to October 17, 1983. It was the first documented comparison of the nesting biology and food habits of Fork-tailed and Leach's Storm-petrels along the BC coast. The research was conducted on a small islet, which we called Petrel Island for convenience. Petrel Island is off Hippa Island, which in turn is a larger island off the west coast of Haida Gwaii. Study results on the nesting biology have been published under the title of "Comparison of nesting biology of Fork-tailed and Leach's Storm-petrels" in *Colonial Waterbirds*,[1] and that of food habits under the title of "The importance of *Paracallisoma coecus* and myctophid fishes to nesting Fork-tailed and Leach's Storm-petrels in the Queen Charlotte Islands, British Columbia" in the *Journal of Plankton Research*.[2]

Leach's Storm-petrel.
(Photo Credit: C. Schlawe, U.S. Fish and Wildlife Service)

Logistics

The logistics for a long and continuous field study along a remote part of BC's coast is challenging. It is like a military operation, except there are no enemies, instead there are physical elements to overcome such as isolation, severe storms, breaking waves, rough landings, and emergencies. Moira Lemon, Michael Rodway, Leo Rankin, R. Reusch and I formed relay teams of two or three persons each to investigate the biology of the storm-petrels over the course of a four-and-a-half-month period. At the end of the study in October, only Leo and I were left on Petrel Island.

Leo spent more time on Petrel Island than any other team member. He took one well deserved month off halfway through the investigation. Teams arrived or left the island by helicopter or Otter seaplane. Landing by seaplane at Petrel Island was difficult because of the swell and breaking of waves and the presence of rocky outcrops along the shore. Seaplanes docked in a sheltered bay off Graham Island, one of the two large islands making up Haida Gwaii, where people and equipment were unloaded. From there a Zodiac, kept on Petrel Island, transported investigators and equipment from Graham Island to Petrel, sea conditions permitting. We engaged a helicopter when there were few passengers or equipment to be transported. The helicopter could land directly on the Petrel Island beach, provided visibility was good. Foggy conditions often prevailed. We used a radiotelephone to communicate with the outside world and in case of emergency.

We slept in small tents, which one entered by crawling on all fours. The tents were firmly anchored to the ground with wooden stakes, ropes, and rocks to prevent storms from blowing them away, which occasionally happened. We used a large tent equipped with a woodstove, called a cook tent, for cooking, eating, warmth, socializing, writing up field observations, conversing by radiotelephone, and shelter from rain and storms, which could last long during dark October days. For further comfort, Leo built a sturdy field toilet where we could relax, with 360-degree views of our surroundings. Although isolated, life was comfortable with our two basic commodities—the cook tent and the toilet.

Storm-petrel Regurgitations

We had no previous experience collecting food samples from storm-petrels. We pioneered new methods and improved them in the process. Adult storm-petrels arrived at the colony between eleven o'clock p.m. and four o'clock a.m. to feed their nestlings in burrows dug into the ground. We captured the adults with a one-inch mesh net, which was strung over tree branches about three or four metres above ground, at the edge of the forest and beach. We anchored the bottom end of the net with boulders from the beach. Beneath the net, we placed a sturdy and transparent plastic groundsheet. When the storm-petrels flew into the net, they regurgitated immediately before we could make them do so in containers, a method used for sampling Cassin's Auklet regurgitations. We used mussel shells found on the beach to scrape regurgitations from the groundsheet. Most regurgitations that dropped on the groundsheet remained intact. Those which scattered we discarded. The combination of the groundsheet on the beach and the scraping of regurgitations with mussel shells were key to our successful collection of food samples from storm-petrels.

Storm-petrel Diet

Twenty-six prey species were identified, of which the amphipod *Paracallisoma coecus* together with small fishes made up most of the prey biomass. *P. coecus*, a bathypelagic (deep water) amphipod, may migrate to the ocean surface at night, where storm-petrels may acquire it. Of the fishes, there was an interesting mix of bathypelagic, mesopelagic, and more shallow-water fishes in the regurgitations. Most of the observed deepwater fishes in the storm-petrel diet migrate to the ocean surface at night. Many possess photophores and are luminescent, which may make these fishes visible to the storm-petrels. Some deepwater fishes, such as the big-eye lantern fish, do not migrate to the surface at night. These fishes may have been acquired by storm-petrels in areas of upwelling. Foods of lesser importance to storm-petrels were copepods, isopods, euphausiids, shrimps, squids, octopus, and jellyfishes. The jellyfish *Velella velella* only occurred in Leach's Storm-petrel's regurgitations, which may reflect that these storm-petrels forage over the open ocean, where *V. velella* occurs most frequently.[2,3] Fork-tailed Storm-petrels, on the other hand, forage mostly over the shelf, shelf break, and in waters not far beyond the shelf.[3] Looking back, I still find our 1983 observations very interesting.

Coast Guard Visit and Preparation for Departure

The Coast Guard paid us a visit in October. Earlier on, we informed them that we needed a new battery for our radiotelephone. The Coast Guard suddenly arrived off Petrel Island on a dark and stormy evening. Leo and I quickly prepared our Zodiac for meeting the ship, which was at some distance offshore. We timed our departure from shore between breaking waves. Fortunately, we arrived at the Coast Guard vessel intact. The crew provided us with a new battery, and we returned to the island. We were overtaken by a huge wave among the rocky outcrops near shore. Shivering and soaking wet, we managed to grab the rope of our boat and pull the Zodiac to the beach. We lost one oar, but were glad that we did not lose the vital battery for our radiotelephone.

During the last days of our investigations, Leo became eager to leave the island. Every other day he would inform me how many Leach's Storm-petrel chicks were still left in our study plot before they would fledge and leave their nest burrows. One day, Leo excitedly said, "There are only six chicks left in the plot." "It is time to leave!" I replied. There was no point to wait for six storm-petrels to fledge over the next two weeks. Based on observed fledging periods, we could calculate their approximate departure from nest burrows. We phoned Sandspit airport and talked to a helicopter pilot. The pilot would pick us up on October 18, weather permitting, but he could not predict the time of day he would arrive. Since we had a few days left, we packed all items for which we had no immediate need. Heavy equipment, such as our Zodiac, gasoline tanks, and outboard motor were stored beneath canvas on Petrel Island. Later on, the equipment was transported to the Institute of Ocean Sciences at Patricia Bay on Vancouver Island.

On the day of departure, we were soundly asleep when the helicopter suddenly and noisily hovered over the beach early in the morning. When the helicopter landed, we raced to prepare for our return to civilization. We flattened the wood stove and chimney pipes and squeezed the damaged cook tent into packs as small as possible. We placed them in a net slung beneath the helicopter together with canned food and other items. The previous day, Leo had sorted the best leftover foods to be stored in his backpack, to the point of bursting. The extra food would provide for him and his girlfriend during their frugal student life.

It was a good sign that the sun shone when we left Petrel Island, although later on I grew apprehensive when we ran into heavy mist banks crossing over mountainous terrain from west to east Haida Gwaii. Fortunately we made it to Sandspit, where we discarded the unusable equipment and gave the canned food in the net to the pilot, who in turn donated the cans to people in need in his community.

Three years later, I read in the local newspaper that my favourite helicopter pilot died during a fatal crash on a flight between Port McNeill and Campbell River on Vancouver Island. He was the main pilot who transported field assistants and me between Port Hardy and Triangle Island during a five-year study of seabirds. I felt sorry for the pilot and his family, but at the same time was grateful that he and other helicopter pilots always flew us safely to and from our island destinations.

Strait of Georgia and other Marine Ecosystems

In 1977, I became a guest scientist at the Institute of Ocean Sciences (IOS) and was given an office there, which meant I didn't have to travel back and forth each weekday from my home in North Saanich by ferry and bus to the CWS office in Delta on the BC mainland. The travel to work from home and back took at least five hours per day, but there was one benefit—that of having the time to write scientific papers undisturbed on the ferry. My new IOS office was only an eight-minute drive from home. However, I still attended CWS main functions and meetings in Delta when necessary.

I was the only CWS guest scientist at IOS, and I much enjoyed the company of other marine scientists. IOS directors and managers strongly supported my research. One time, Cedric Mann, the IOS director, called me to his office and said: "Kees, we are happy to have you at the institute, and to have a CWS scientist as a guest. If we can be of any assistance at all, let me know." I was surprised by Cedric's remark, but what a surprise it was to be appreciated! Because of IOS support, I had ready access to IOS coxswains and boats for studies in the Strait of Georgia.

Study of Active Pass Upwelling

During my year-round ferry travel through Active Pass between Swartz Bay and Tsawwassen, I observed large numbers of small-sized gulls, such as Bonaparte's and Mew Gulls feeding at distinct seasonal time periods near an upwelling at the western end of Active Pass. The upwelling is caused when the tidal stream is deflected upward by the bottom topography within the Active Pass confined channel. When present, the upwelling can be seen at the surface as a domed patch of smooth water containing intermittent boils.

Much has been written about the interrelation between seabirds and large-scale oceanic upwelling, which is brought about by winds and the Coriolis force driving surface water offshore, while those waters are being replaced by relatively slow upwelling of cool and nutrient-rich subsurface waters. However, at that time, no serious studies had been made of the relationship between marine birds and fast tidal upwelling, where zooplankton near the bottom is brought to the surface within a few minutes. Having IOS support for coxswains and boats and close contact with physical oceanographers and zooplankton specialists, I could not pass up the opportunity of investigating the relationship between the Active Pass upwelling and the two gull species.

In the ensuing study, my co-workers and I investigated the close interrelation of bottom topography, tidal phases, water temperatures, salinity, the appearance of zooplankton on the surface, as well as the timing of the feeding of the two gull species on the concentrated zooplankton in the small scale and tidal upwelling zone in Active Pass during one complete annual cycle.[1] My companions were Ildy Szabo, a zooplankton specialist, and Dick Herlinveaux, an IOS technician, who volunteered to help with plankton tows and measurements of salinity and surface temperatures. Ildy, Dick, and I collected the data by boat in Active Pass, and had much fun doing it, while passengers onboard passing ferries waved to us. Later on, Paul Greisman, a physical oceanographer, assisted with interpreting the physical oceanographic data we collected. The study showed that an interdisciplinary approach can break into new areas of research, and be fruitful and fun at the same time.

We observed that the largest numbers of feeding gulls coincided with high densities of amphipod prey in fall (September and October) and euphausiid prey in spring (February through May) at the upwelling zone. Both species of gulls avoided large planktonic forms such as hydromedusae, ctenophores, siphonores, larvaceans, and chaetognaths, as well as small planktonic crustaceans such as cladocerans, ostracods, barnacle nauplii, and small copepods. That crustaceans such as euphausiids and amphipods are preyed upon by gulls while other planktonic forms are neglected, may be related to the high energy content of those crustaceans.

Parathemisto pacifica, the most common amphipod eaten by the Bonaparte's Gulls in Active Pass, had large purple-black eyes and purple spots on all dorsal somites. Red blood pigments could be easily seen in each somite. The high frequency of that amphipod in the gull diet probably relates to both its high density in the upwelling zone as well as its visibility. The euphausiids eaten by the gulls also had conspicuous black eyes and pink body pigmentation.

Outside Active Pass and other tidally active localities, the two gull species fed mostly on fishes and intertidal organisms. Because of the thousands of gulls utilizing the upwelling site for food, Active Pass is considered to be a very important feeding location for Bonaparte's Gulls in spring and again in autumn, and for Mew Gulls in early spring. There are other tidal upwelling sites, such as Porlier Pass and Skookumchuck Narrows in the Strait of Georgia region, where the two gull species concentrate, but none is as spectacular and of the magnitude as Active Pass.[1]

Besides zooplankton, Pacific hake, a benthic fish, were observed to pop to the surface in the upwelling zone at Active Pass. Swim bladders were seen protruding through the mouths of dying hake, suggesting death by gas embolism. Bald Eagles fed upon these hake by seizing the fish with their talons at the water's surface. The eagles anticipated the appearance of hake at the upwelling site, as many eagles lined up in trees along Active Pass, one or two hours in advance of the appearance of hake. That suggests that the eagles knew when their meal would be served. I never missed an opportunity during my frequent ferry travel through Active Pass to see what new and exciting things were going on there!

Strait of Georgia Symposium and the Importance of Baseline Data

In 1987, I organized a symposium on the Strait of Georgia with Rob Butler, a CWS colleague. The symposium, entitled: "The ecology and status of marine and shoreline birds in the Strait of Georgia, British Columbia" was a success, and was published as a Special Publication of the Canadian Wildlife Service.[2] In anticipation of the symposium, I organized censuses and studies of nesting seabirds, such as Glaucous-winged Gulls, Double-crested and Pelagic Cormorants, and Pigeon Guillemots, as well as of shoreline birds such as Black Oystercatchers and Bald Eagles in the Strait with help of IOS coxswains and boats. Rob added his expertise on Great Blue Herons and estuarine and shorebirds.

Other CWS biologists and Ken Morgan, my main contractor stationed at IOS, contributed in different capacities. Besides CWS staff, there were participants from various disciplines in the Department of Fisheries and Oceans and from different universities. There had been a 1983 symposium on the fisheries and oceanography of the Strait of Georgia, but that one did not include information on marine and shoreline birds, despite the fact that such birds occupy high trophic levels in the Strait's aquatic food web.

In the final chapter of the symposium, Rob and I made half a dozen recommendations, mostly on what marine bird habitat should be secured and protected. Strangely, we did not make any recommendation on continuing with the gathering of baseline data on marine and shoreline birds in the Strait, perhaps because we had just completed such an exercise. I had benefited from a seabird catalogue compiled by Rudi Drent and Charles Guiguet, which showed trends of nesting populations of Glaucous-winged Gulls and Double-crested and Pelagic Cormorants in some colonies, one of which was on Mandarte Island.[3] Although the catalogue contained mostly anecdotal data, Rudi's efforts made a deep impression on me because of his organizing skills and dedication to the subject. He collected all that information, with the help of Charles, during his spare time as a student at the University of British Columbia. Rudi later became a well-known and honored professor at the University of Groningen in the Netherlands.

I hope that Rob's and my efforts of bringing together baseline information and research on marine and shoreline birds in the Strait of Georgia will be continued by the Canadian Wildlife Service. It is one of the least expensive and most accessible marine ecosystems (in CWS front yard) to monitor. The data presented by the symposium participants can be easily built upon by future investigations and symposia. Only then will we be able to see changes and trends in marine and shoreline bird populations and improve our understanding of causes behind these changes.

Besides the Strait of Georgia, the ecology, status and conservation of marine and shoreline birds were investigated on the west coast of Vancouver Island and in Haida Gwaii.[4,5] Although the threats to birds in these three regions were often the same, they differed in magnitude. The greatest threat to birds in the Strait of Georgia was from loss of estuarine habitat through development. On the west coast of Vancouver Island, the main threats were the oiling of birds and the destruction of Marbled Murrelet nesting habitat caused by logging of old - growth forests. In Haida Gwaii, introduced predators such as rats, devastated several Ancient Murrelet nesting colonies, while racoons destroyed those of Rhinoceros and Cassin's Auklets.[6] As with the Strait of Georgia, on-going baseline data and research on bird populations on the west coast of Vancouver Island, and in Haida Gwaii are necessary to protect and conserve the marine bird resources in these ecosystems.

The ecology and status of marine and shoreline birds in the Strait of Georgia, British Columbia.

Kees Vermeer

Kees Vermeer
Robert W. Butler
Ken H. Morgan
(editors)

The ecology, status, and conservation of marine and shoreline birds on the west coast of Vancouver Island

Occasional Paper
Number 75
Canadian Wildlife Service

Environment Canada / Environnement Canada
Canadian Wildlife Service / Service canadien de la faune

The ecology, status, and conservation of marine and shoreline birds on the west coast of Vancouver Island.

Immigrant Gone to Heaven

Kees Vermeer
Ken H. Morgan
(editors)

The ecology, status, and conservation of marine and shoreline birds of the Queen Charlotte Islands

Occasional Paper
Number 93
Canadian Wildlife Service

Canadä

Environment Canada
Canadian Wildlife Service

Environnement Canada
Service canadien de la faune

The ecology, status, and conservation of marine and shoreline birds of the Queen Charlotte Islands (now Haida Gwaii).

Kees Vermeer

Monitoring Birds of the Fraser River Estuary

Smaller BC ecosystems, such as estuaries, have some of the highest concentrations of aquatic bird species and populations. One example is the Fraser River delta, the largest and most important estuary in British Columbia, where in some years, as many as 1.4 million birds (mostly waterfowl and shorebirds) use the estuary or migrate through it.[7] These bird populations will be vulnerable to potential major oil spills whenever tanker traffic increases significantly from Burrard Inlet and turns southward from there into the Strait of Georgia with the Gulf Islands on one side and the Fraser River delta on the other.

Bird populations in the Fraser River delta where for the first time year-round (March 1988 – February 1989) surveyed by seventeen teams of observers of the Vancouver Natural History Society (VNHS) who walked the dikes near high tidelines and recorded all bird species seen through binoculars or telescopes. The authors of the first chapter of a report on 'The abundance and distribution of estuarine birds in the Strait of Georgia, British Columbia' analyzed the VNHS data and reported that of all birds, shorebirds and waterfowl were far the most numerous, whereas loons, grebes, cormorants, alcids, and herons made up only relatively small proportions.[7] They also found that the Fraser River delta intertidal zone had far more migrant and wintering shorebirds, and higher densities of wintering ducks and geese, than other British Columbia estuaries. These numerous visitors to the delta were attributed to a rich supply of food over a vast expanse of intertidal mudflats, and to the presence of large tracks of nearby farmlands.

The authors recommended that since estuaries and nearby farmlands constitute important feeding habitats for shorebirds and waterbirds, that both habitats should be preserved.[7] Furthermore, they recommended that accurate boat censuses of estuarine bird populations should be conducted for reliable baseline information and monitoring as both aerial and ground surveys were found to have major shortcomings.[7] The latter recommendation was made as year-round and more accurate censuses of estuarine bird species and populations were conducted by one of the authors and one experienced bird watcher in a shallow-draft boat at high tide throughout shallow intertidal zones in five estuaries along the southeast coast of Vancouver Island in 1989.[7]

Immigrant Gone to Heaven

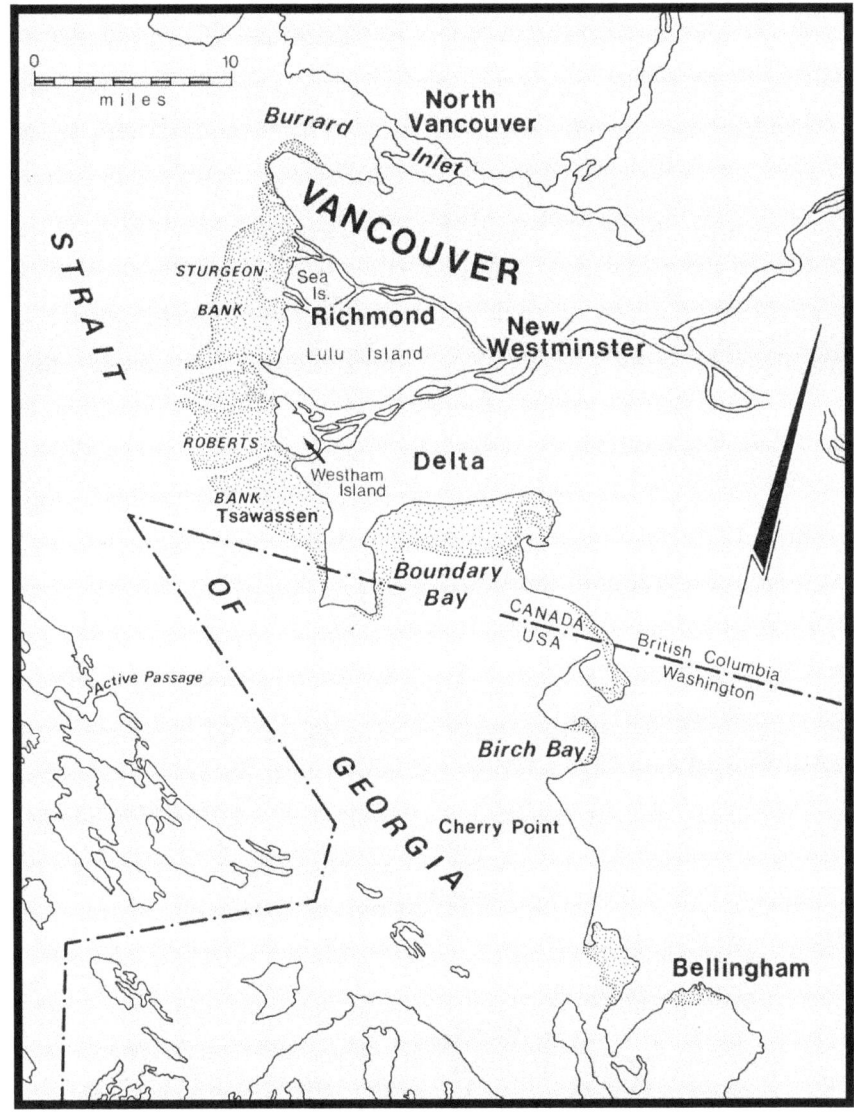

The Fraser River Delta – Intertidal zone at Sturgeon and Roberts Banks, and Boundary Bay. Taken from: Vermeer K, Vermeer R (1975) Oil threat to birds on the Canadian west coast. *Canadian Field Naturalist* 89:278-298.

Even though the Fraser River estuary has been recognized internationally as a significant Important Bird and Biodiversity Area, and globally as a significant Western Hemispheric Shorebird Network site, the estuarine bird populations and their feeding habitat will remain vulnerable to potential shipping terminal expansion, oil spillage and other forms of human disturbance and destruction. I hope the Vancouver Natural History Society (presently Nature Vancouver) continues its splendid initiative to conduct year-round bird surveys with improved census methods. Reliable censuses are necessary to determine population trends and can play an important role in the management and preservation of a unique estuarine bird community at the edge of the city of Vancouver.

The abundance and distribution of estuarine birds in the Strait of Georgia, British Columbia.

Marine Birds of the Temperate North Pacific

In 1990, I led an international symposium in which participants documented the status, ecology, and distribution of marine birds of the temperate North Pacific, which is the largest marine ecosystem I came to be involved with. The symposium was held at the Royal British Columbia Museum in Victoria on 22-23 February of that year. The symposium proceedings entitled *The status, ecology, and conservation of marine birds of the North Pacific* were edited by me and co-editors Ken Briggs, Ken Morgan and Douglas Siegel-Causey. They were published by the Canadian Wildlife Service in a special publication for the Pacific Seabird Group and BC Ministry of Environment, Lands and Parks in 1993.[8] Thirty-eight participants from the United States of America, seven from Canada, four from Russia, two from Japan, two from New Zealand, and one each from Mexico and the United Kingdom, participated in the proceedings. These numbers show that the American marine ornithologists as symposium contributors were a force to be reckoned with. Of the Americans, one third were Alaskans.

The contents of the symposium proceedings were described by the editors as follows:

> These proceedings consist of three sections: (1) Bird distribution at sea as determined by physical and biological processes, (2) Status, ecology, and conservation of nesting and visiting seabirds, and (3) Environmental hazards to seabirds. The first section describes the distribution of birds at sea in relation to physical and biological processes in the Bering Sea, in the central North Pacific, off the coasts of British Columbia and Washington, and in the California Current, and explores the effects of climatic changes, such as the El Niño/Southern Oscillation and potential global warming, on seabirds and their prey.

> The second section includes chapters on both nesting and visiting seabirds in the North Pacific, from the Tropic of Cancer in the south to the Bering Sea in the north. Bird groups covered albatrosses, fulmars, gadfly petrels and storm-petrels, shearwaters, gulls, kittiwakes, terns, guillemots, murrelets, murres, puffins, and auklets. The third section includes chapters on the effects of environmental hazards such as gillnetting, introduced predators, human disturbance, plastic ingestion, contamination by trace metals and chlorinated hydrocarbons, and oil spillage on marine birds.
>
> Individual chapters include recommendations on necessary future studies and actions to protect seabirds. Although the chapters and sections vary in scope and depth, this book provides the most recent overview of what is known of the status, ecology, and distribution of marine birds of the temperate North Pacific. **We hope that these proceedings will become an important reference for ornithologists and managers, and that decision makers will act on the recommendations so that North Pacific marine birds and their biological environment may be preserved.**

Thirty years after the symposium, the same hope can be expressed for the preservation of North Pacific marine birds and their environment.

Immigrant Gone to Heaven

Edited by
Kees Vermeer,
Kenneth T. Briggs,
Ken H. Morgan, and
Douglas Siegel-Causey

The status, ecology, and conservation of marine birds of the North Pacific

**Special Publication
Canadian Wildlife Service**

Published by the Canadian Wildlife Service for the Pacific Seabird Group and the British Columbia Ministry of Environment, Lands and Parks.

Environment Canada — Environnement Canada
Canadian Wildlife Service — Service canadien de la faune

The status, ecology, and conservation of marine birds of the North Pacific.

References

Pleas for Protection of Fish-eating Bird Colonies

1. Vermeer K (1969) Colonies of Double-crested Cormorants and White Pelicans in Alberta. *Canadian Field-Naturalist* 83:36–39.

2. Farley FL (1922) Summer birds of the Lac La Biche and Fort McMurray region. *Canadian Field-Naturalist* 36:72–75.

3. Soper JD (1952) Protection of wildfowl breeding grounds in the Lake Newell locality, Eastern Irrigation District, Alberta, Canadian Wildlife Service, Edmonton.

4. Vermeer K (1970) Colonies of Double-crested Cormorants and White Pelicans in Saskatchewan. *Canadian Field-Naturalist* 84:39–42.

5. Carson RD (1966) Destruction of colonial birds on an island on Suggi Lake. *Blue Jay* 24:96–97.

6. Houston CS (1962) Hazards faced by colonial birds. *Blue Jay* 20:74–77.

7. Vermeer K (1970) Distribution and size of colonies of White Pelicans *(Pelecanus erythrorhyncos)* in Canada. *Canadian Journal of Zoology* 48:1029–1032.

8. Blokpoel H (1971) Fox predation on a bird island. *Blue Jay* 29:32–34.

9. Vermeer K (1969) The present status of Double-crested Cormorants in Manitoba. *Blue Jay* 27:217–220.

10. McLeod JA, Bondar GF (1953) A brief study of the Double-crested Cormorant on Lake Winnipegosis. *Canadian Field-Naturalist* 67:1–11.

11. Vermeer K (1970) Some aspects of the nesting of Double-crested Cormorants at Cypress Lake, Saskatchewan in 1969. A plea for protection. *Blue Jay* 28:11–13.

12. Vermeer K (1970) Aquatic park proposal for Lake Winnipegosis, Kawinaw and Pelican Lakes. *Blue Jay* 28:66–67.

13. Vermeer K (1971) The Pelican-protection or extinction. *Canadian Audubon* 33:103–104.

14. Vermeer K, Rankin L (1984) Population trends in nesting Double-crested and Pelagic Cormorants in Canada. *Murrelet* 65:1–9.

15. Vermeer K (1969) Great Blue Heron colonies in Alberta. *Canadian Field-Naturalist* 83:237–242.

16. Vermeer K, Anweiler GC (1970) Great Blue Heron colonies in Saskatchewan in 1970. *Blue Jay* 28:158–161.

17. Vermeer K (1970) Insular Great Blue Heron colonies on large Manitoba Lakes. *Blue Jay* 28:84–86.

18. Vermeer K, Hatch DRM (1972) Additional information on Great Blue Heron colonies in Manitoba. *Blue Jay* 30:89–92.

19. Vermeer K (1973) Great Blue Heron and Double-crested Cormorant colonies in the prairie provinces. *Canadian Field-Naturalist* 87:427–432.

20. Houston CS (1963) R. F. Oldaker, the man who reads gull bands with a telescope. *Blue Jay* 21:53–57.

Pursuing the Trail of Pesticides and Mercury in Aquatic Birds

1. Vermeer K, Windsor JA (1971) Spotted Sandpipers as possible indicators of mercury contamination of rivers. *Blue Jay* 29:59–60.

2. Vermeer K, Reynolds LM (1970) Organochlorine residues in aquatic birds in the Canadian prairie provinces. *Canadian Field-Naturalist* 84:117–130.

3. Vermeer K, Risebrough RW (1972) Additional information on egg shell thickness in relation to DDE concentrations in Great Blue Heron eggs. *Canadian Field-Naturalist* 86:384–385.

4. Hickey JJ, Anderson DW (1968) Chlorinated hydrocarbons and egg shell changes in raptorial and fish-eating birds. *Science* 162:271–273.

5. Fyfe RW, Campbell J, Hayson B, Hodson K (1969) Regional population declines and organochlorine insecticides in Canadian Prairie Falcons. *Canadian Field-Naturalist* 83:191–200.

6. Heath RG, Spann JW, Freitzer JF (1969) Marked DDE impairment of Mallard reproduction in controlled studies. *Nature* 224:47–48.

7. Vermeer K (1971) A survey of mercury residues in aquatic bird eggs in the Canadian prairie provinces. *Transactions of the North American Wildlife and Natural Resources Conference* 36:138–152.

8. Vermeer K, Armstrong FAJ (1972) Correlation between mercury in wing and breast muscles in ducks. *Journal of Wildlife Management* 36:1270–1273.

9. Vermeer K, Armstrong FAJ, Hatch DRM (1973) Mercury in aquatic birds at Clay Lake, Western Ontario. *Journal of Wildlife Management* 37:58–61.

10. Vermeer K (1972) The crayfish *Orconectis virilis* as an indicator of mercury contamination. *Canadian Field-Naturalist* 86:123–125.

11. Vermeer K, Risebrough RW, Spaans AL, Reynolds LM (1974) Pesticide effects on fishes and birds in rice fields of Surinam, South America. *Environmental Pollution* 7:217–236.

12. Godfrey WE (1966) The birds of Canada. Queen's Printer and Controller of Stationary. Ottawa, Canada.

13. Spaans AL (2003) Coastal birds of Suriname. Foundation for Nature Conservation in Suriname. Paramaribo, Suriname.

Back to Seabirds in British Columbia

1. Vermeer K, Vermeer R (1975) Oil threat to birds on the Canadian west coast. *Canadian Field-Naturalist* 89:278–298.

Seabird Studies and Tragedy on Triangle Island

1. Vermeer K, Manuwal DA, Bingham DS (1976) Birds observed at Triangle Island. *Murrelet* 57:35–42.

2. Vermeer K (1979) Nesting requirements, food and breeding distribution of Rhinoceros Auklets *(Cerorhinca monocerata)* and Tufted Puffins *(Lunda cirrhata) Ardea* 67:101–110.

3. Vermeer K, Vermeer RA, Summers KR, Billings RB (1979) Number and habitat selection of Cassin's Auklet breeding on Triangle Island, British Columbia. *Auk* 96:143–151.

4. Rodway MS, Lemon MJF and Summers KR (1992) Seabird breeding populations in the Scott Islands on the west coast of Vancouver Island. Pages 52–59 in Vermeer K, Butler RW, Morgan KH (editors) The ecology, status and conservation of marine and

shoreline birds on the west coast of Vancouver Island., *Canadian Wildlife Service Occasional Paper* No. 75, Ottawa.

5. Vermeer K, Sealy SG, Lemon MJF, Rodway MS (1984) Predation and potential environmental perturbances on Ancient Murrelets nesting in British Columbia. Pages 757–770 in Croxall JP, Evans PGH, Schreiber RW (editors) Status and conservation of the world's seabirds, *ICBP Technical Publication* No. 2, Norwich, England.

6. Vermeer K, Westerheim SJ (1984) Fish changes in diets of Rhinoceros Auklets and their implications. Pages 96–105 in Nettleship DN, Sanger GA, Springer PF (editors) Marine birds: their feeding ecology and commercial fisheries relationships, *Canadian Wildlife Service Special Publication*, Ottawa.

7. Vermeer K (1982) The importance of timing and type of prey to reproductive success of Rhinoceros Auklet *(Cerorhinca monocerata) Ibis* 122:343–350.

8. Vermeer K, Cullen L, Porter M (1979) A provisional explanation of the reproductive failure of Tufted Puffins *Lunda cirrhata* on Triangle Island, British Columbia. *Ibis* 121:348–353.

Rhinoceros Auklet Fish-sampling Expeditions

1. Vermeer K, Westerheim SJ (1984) Fish changes in diets of nestling Rhinoceros Auklets and their implications. Pages 69–105 in Nettleship DN, Sanger SG, Springer PF (editors) Marine birds: Their feeding ecology and commercial fisheries relationships. *Canadian Wildlife Service Special Publication*, Ottawa.

Cassin's Auklets as Monitors of Zooplankton and Climate Change

1. Vermeer K (1985) A five-year summary (1978–1982) of the nestling diet of Cassin's Auklets in British Columbia. *Canadian Technical Report of Hydrography and Ocean Sciences.* No. 56.

2. Vermeer K (1984) The diet and food composition of nestling Cassin's Auklets during summer, and a comparison with other plankton-feeding alcids. *Murrelet* 65:65–77.

3. Miller CB, Frost BW, Batchelder HP, Clemons MJ, Conway RE (1984) Life histories of large grazing copepods in a sub-arctic ocean gyre: *Neocalanus plumchrus, Neocalanus cristatus* and *Eucalanus bungii* in the Northeast Pacific. *Progress in Oceanography* 13:201–243.

4. Vermeer K (1981) The importance of plankton to breeding Cassin's Auklets. *Journal of Plankton Research* 3:315–329.

5. Vermeer K, Vermeer RA, Summers KR and Billings RR (1979) Numbers and habitat selection of Cassin's Auklet on Triangle Island, British Columbia. *Auk* 96:143-151.

6. Fulton J, Arai MN, Mason JC (1982) Euphausiids, coelenterates, ctenophores and other zooplankton from the Canadian Pacific Coast Ichthyoplankton Survey, 1980. *Canadian Technical Report of Fisheries and Aquatic Sciences* No. 1125.

7. Vermeer K (1992) The diet of birds as a tool for monitoring the biological environment. Pages 41–50 in Vermeer K, Butler RW, Morgan KH (editors). The ecology, status and conservation of marine and shoreline birds on the west coast of Vancouver Island. *Canadian Wildlife Service Occasional Paper* No. 75.

8. Vermeer K, Cullen L, Porter M (1979) A provisional explanation of the reproductive failure of Tufted Puffins *Lunda cirrhata* on Triangle Island, British Columbia. *Ibis* 121:348–354.

Storm-petrels in Haida Gwaii

1. Vermeer K, Devito K, Rankin L (1988) Comparison of nesting biology of Fork-tailed and Leach's Storm-Petrels. *Colonial Waterbirds* 11:46–57.

2. Vermeer K, Devito K (1988) The importance of *Paracallisoma coecus* and myctophid fishes to nesting Fork-tailed and Leach's Storm-Petrels in the Queen Charlotte Islands, British Columbia. *Journal of Plankton Research* 10:63–75.

3. Vermeer K, Rankin L (1984) Pelagic seabird populations in Hecate Strait and Queen Charlotte Sound: comparison with the west coast of the Queen Charlotte Islands. *Canadian Technical Report of Hydrography and Ocean Sciences* No. 52, Institute of Ocean Sciences, Sidney, BC.

Strait of Georgia and other Marine Ecosystems

1. Vermeer K, Szabo I, Greisman P (1987) The relationship between plankton-feeding Bonaparte's and Mew Gulls and tidal upwelling at Active Pass, British Columbia. *Journal of Plankton Research* 9:483–501.

2. Vermeer K, Butler RW, editors (1989) The ecology and status of marine and shoreline birds in the Strait of Georgia, British Columbia. *Canadian Wildlife Service Special Publication*, Ottawa.

3. Drent RH, Guiguet CJ (1961) A catalogue of British Columbia seabird colonies. *Occasional Papers of the British Columbia Provincial Museum* No.12, Victoria.

4. Vermeer K, Butler RW, Morgan KH, editors (1992) The ecology, status and conservation of marine and shoreline birds on the west coast of Vancouver Island. *Canadian Wildlife Service Occasional Paper* No. 75, Ottawa.

5. Vermeer K, Morgan KH, editors (1997) The ecology, status and conservation of marine and shoreline birds of the Queen Charlotte Islands. *Canadian Wildlife Service Occasional Paper* No. 93, Ottawa.

6. Harfenist A, Kaiser GW (1997) Effects on introduced predators on the nesting seabirds of the Queen Charlotte Islands. Pages 132-136 in Vermeer K, Morgan KH (editors) The ecology, status and conservation of marine and shoreline birds of the Queen Charlotte Islands. *Canadian Wildlife Service Occasional Paper* No. 93, Ottawa.

7. Butler RW, Vermeer K, editors (1994) The abundance and distribution of estuarine birds in the Strait of Georgia, British Columbia. *Canadian Wildlife Service Occasional Paper* No. 83, Ottawa.

8. Vermeer K, Briggs KT, Morgan KH, Siegel-Causey D, editors (1993) The status, ecology, and conservation of marine birds of the North Pacific. *Canadian Wildlife Service Special Publication*, Ottawa.

PART III
Reminiscences of Youth and World War II

Every now and then, during my life in Canada, I journeyed to Holland to spend time with my Dutch family and visit familiar places, such as Noordeloos, where I was born, and Gorinchem, where I lived as a teenager during World War II. These visits stirred up memories. Two of my World War II stories, "Our Family Adapts to the German Occupation" and "Memories of the Liberation of Gorinchem" were previously published in the *Dutch in Wartime* series by Tom Bijvoet.

Early Years in Noordeloos

My early years were spent in Noordeloos (Without North), where my father was the principal of a Christian school. Noordeloos is a small village, founded around 1025 AD, in the Ablasserwaard in the province of South Holland. We lived in an old schoolhouse where my father received his coffee, while teaching a class, through a small door in the wall that connected to our living quarters. Our family consisted of four boys and two girls, of which I was the youngest. There was an eleven-year age gap between me and my brother Jan, the next youngest sibling. Two siblings had been born in the eleven-year interval, but had died. According to my family, one died of the English Disease (probably rickets) and the other of the German Disease (probably measles).

My family in 1931. (L–R) Cato, Jan, Father, Ali, Mother with Kees
(not in the photo: Wim and Gijs)

**Vermeer family in 1919.
(L–R) Father, Ali, Cato, Wim, Mother with Jan, Gijs**

Schoolhouse in Noordeloos.

Vermeer family home at back of schoolhouse, autumn 1966. Brother Jan with daughters Caroline and Wil.

Years of Economic Crisis

The time I grew up in Noordeloos (1930–1938) was a difficult one economically. My eldest brothers Wim and Gijs, who were twenty and seventeen years older than me, respectively, could not find jobs and spent most of their time at home. My father did not like that and contacted the municipal secretary, whom he knew well. He asked if Gijs could work at the municipal office as a volunteer. The secretary accepted my father's offer, and Gijs became an assistant clerk. At the end of his first two months at the office, Gijs was paid ten guilders for his service. Gijs was floating on a cloud after he found a paying job, while others could not find any. However, after finishing his third month at the municipal office, he was not paid the ten guilders. He walked restlessly around the office until the municipal clerk in charge of finances asked him, "Gijs, why are you so restless?" Gijs responded, "Where are my ten guilders? I earned it, and it is the end of the month!" "Listen, Gijs, I need to tell you something," said the clerk. "Your father did not provide the ten guilders for you this time." When Gijs understood the situation, he fell into despair.

On a certain day, a young teacher, who had just finished his teacher training program, arrived on a bicycle in Noordeloos from Giessendam. He asked my father for a job at his school, and mentioned that he would love to teach, even if he was not paid a salary. My father, who could use an extra teacher, accepted the offer. The name of the new teacher was Teun Brand. Teun cycled every school day from Giessendam to Noordeloos, which is thirteen kilometres away. After half a year, Teun's biking pants had worn out, and his parents did not have the money to pay for new ones. Teun asked my father for help. My father advised Teun to visit the school board members and explain his dilemma to them. He followed my father's advice, and was successful in his request. Teun's new pants were paid for with school money.

(L–R) Front: Sister Cato, Kees, Father;
Standing: Three teachers, with Teun Brand in the centre

My Old Friend Klaas

Across the road from the schoolhouse lived my old friend Klaas van Drenth, to whom I brought my mother's potato peelings regularly for his rabbits. Klaas eked out a living by transporting goods with a small boat. He would travel with his boat to Gorinchem, a small city about seven kilometres away, and would be gone for several days. When he returned, he would bring me a few cookies with coloured sweet glaze on top. That was all he could afford to give.

On April 2, 1934, when I was nearly four years old, I brought potato peelings to Klaas in a basket. I was accompanied by a younger friend, Stien Rietveld. Stien also lived across the road from the schoolhouse, and next to Klaas. When we entered Klaas's house, he and his wife Drieke were seated in their chairs. I handed the basket to Klaas. He stood up and said, "Thank you," while combing the peelings with one hand. Then he swayed and fell flat on the hardened ground floor. He still held the basket in his hand, while the peelings scattered over the ground. Drieke stood up from her chair and knelt over Klaas's dead body and said, "Oh mijn jochie, mijn jochie" (Oh my little boy) while gently patting his face. I grabbed the empty basket and ran out of the house with Stien.

Klaas was a small, nice old man. To Drieke, Klaas was her "Jochie." A few days after he died, Klaas's body was transported to the cemetery behind the old Dutch Reformed Church in the village centre. I recall the black-draped horses in front of the black coach, which carried his coffin. Drieke and the coachmen were also dressed in black. The bell in the church tower rang a depressing "Bong … bong … bong …" To me, it sounded as though the bell was ringing forever! Everything was so dark and sombre, the horses, the coach, the dress, and the mood of the people in the village. I felt the effects deep in my little stomach. My old friend Klaas was gone and never to return.

Noordeloos village centre as seen from the church tower where the bell rang for my old friend Klaas.

Noordeloos centre with bridge over Boezem, autumn 1966.

Noordeloos's Gathering Centre

In the centre of Noordeloos, there is an elevated bridge crossing a small river called "boezem" or "Noordeloos," from which the village derived its name. People gathered at the centre whenever there was an important event, such as the queen's birthday. Noordeloos really could feast and there was a committee to organize festivities. There was a well-established band with musicians, called the "Volharding" (Perseverance); and a sturdy music stand with a roof, where the band played popular Dutch songs. Men in the audience smoked their cigars heavily, which were adorned with beautiful bands showing Dutch kings and heroes with fancy hats, owls, and other figures.

I still remember the last morning I spent with my family in Noordeloos in 1938, the day after such a festival. Several of my young friends, including Stien, went with me to the centre where the festivities had taken place. They collected all the cigar bands they could find, but instead of keeping them, they gave them to me. It was their token of friendship and farewell. I pasted them in a small album, which I took with me to Gorinchem.

At one time, there had been a water pump with a lantern on top at the centre, where the people of Noordeloos acquired their water and shared the latest news. My brother Jan painted that scene. I still have one of Jan's painting of that scene, which he brought with him when he visited us in Canada in 1980. Surrounding the Noordeloos centre were stores where our family bought groceries from the Steenis family, bread from baker Hoeijenbos, and candies from the little shop of Pietje Dingemans. Pietje's shop was where all the children in the village wanted to go. She sold bubble gum, licorice (zoethout), licorice shoe laces (veterdrop) and caramels. I would blow up the bubble gum in fiery colors of red, green, and blue. And ah! the caramels. It was not just the caramels I was after, but the little strip of paper tucked inside the caramel wrapper, announcing whether you had won a prize. Sometimes, it was just another caramel. But once in a while, I hit the jackpot and won a basket of chocolate-coated eggs.

Dominating the centre in height was the tall house of the local medical doctor, who treated his patients at their home, and a little bit farther away, the tower of the Dutch Reformed Church, from which the bell rang for my old friend Klaas. The Dutch Reformed Church dates back to the fourteenth century and was at one time a Roman Catholic Church, called Holy Bonefacius Church.

Going to School

I went to school at the age of six. I recall Annie van Zwol teaching me to read my first word on my first day of school. On the blackboard, she wrote: "O," then another "O," after which we read aloud *oo*. Then she added an "M." The first word I could read was *Oom*, meaning uncle.

I and some others came to school in klompen (wooden shoes), which were made by a klompen maker in the village. We stored the klompen in the school hallway before entering the classroom. We were given a slate and a slate-pencil. The slate-pencil was for writing on the slate, which was cleaned with a sponge and a little washcloth. Both the sponge and cloth were stored in a small box. We learned to read from schoolbooks with interesting prints and rhymes, such as:

> A is de aap die eet uit zijn poot
> (the monkey who eats from his paw)
>
> B is de bakker die bakt voor ons brood
> (the baker who bakes bread for us)

Later we wrote with a pen, which we dipped into an inkpot on our desk. When I started my second year in Teun Brand's class, I had to write the above rhyme. That writing is still in my possession. Lately, I noticed I had misspelled a few words, and exchanged both the 'b' for bakker and the 'b' in bakt with a 'k.' That changes the meaning of that rhyme considerably.

Next to the school was a large schoolyard with chestnut trees, where we played games such as catch me if you can, hide-and-seek, and "knikkeren" (a game with marbles). The girls skipped ropes to the tunes of old songs. We looked forward to the queen's birthday when we were treated with lemonade, candies, chocolates, and cookies, and played competitive games such as fishing for apples from a pail of water with your mouth, and racing in a potato sack across the schoolyard. During the winter holidays, Stien and I enjoyed skating over the frozen boezem across the schoolyard.

Immigrant Gone to Heaven

Grades 1 and 2, Noordeloos, 1937.
Kees at far right of front row with klompen (wooden shoes).

Churches of Noordeloos

Noordeloos had three Protestant churches, which was remarkable for a small community. They were the Dutch Reformed, Christian Reformed and the Reformed Church. They all played a role in managing the Christian school, which sometimes led to disagreements. When my father was nominated for school principal in November 1919, the Reformed Church school board members protested against his nomination, because my father belonged to the Christian Reformed Church. The Reformed Church members felt so strongly about my father's nomination, because they were the only ones of the three reformed churches who paid for the building of the Christian school.

For us boys, it was not always easy to have all those different "reformed" eyes watching us. We were not supposed to ride our bikes on Sunday, because it was a rest day. There were many other things we were not supposed to do. My father, a practical person, advised us to play in the polder on Sundays and do whatever we enjoyed. Reformers would not be watching us there on Sunday. We followed his advice, and we did a lot of things in the Dutch polder the Reformers would have never approved of. Perhaps I need to thank the Reformers for their Sunday restrictions, which led to my early interest and love for nature.

Kees in Noordeloos polder.

Selling Clothes and Textiles Door-to-door

Gijs and Wim, who could not find jobs, finally created their own with the help of my mother. She was good-hearted, but could be tough when necessary. My mother suggested to my two brothers that they try to sell clothes for a living. She helped my brothers with the packing of suitcases with clothes and other textiles. Gijs and Wim loaded the suitcases onto their bicycles and off they went. It must have been a difficult task to sell from door-to-door, as they often found excuses not to leave the house. Either it rained, or they said people were doing their laundry and would not have time to buy. But my mother was adamant, and sent them on the road, come what may. They gradually acquired more sales experience. By the time my father retired and our family left Noordeloos for Gorinchem in 1938, Gijs had established a textile store in a neighbouring village called Hoornaar, and Wim had set one up in neighbouring Meerkerk. Both were doing well until World War II started in 1940. But that is another story.

Our Family Adapts to the German Occupation

During the first years of the German occupation of the Netherlands from 1940 to 1943, the Dutch tried to carry on with life as normally as possible. In 1943, when the war started to turn against the Germans, food shortages grew worse, as most of the Dutch grain and dairy products were transported to Germany. My family lived in Gorinchem, then a small city of about fifteen thousand inhabitants, situated on the Merwede river. Gorinchem is surrounded by earthen city walls and gates from the 1600s, which are still beautifully preserved.

In 1943, I was twelve and lived with my retired parents, two sisters, Cato and Ali, and my brother Jan (all in their twenties) on a street called Emmastraat. It was part of a suburb called the Nieuwe Hoven, which was located outside the city walls.

Since my father was a well-liked retired school principal from Noordeloos, a small village in the Alblasserwaard, we had ready access to dairy products from the farmers there. My sisters and I often biked to Noordeloos to buy milk, butter, and cheese. Because of this fortunate access to a good supply of dairy, we also shared with neighbours in dire need. One neighbour was a Jewish woman across the street, who had to wear a yellow star, and hardly dared to come out of her house because of the risk of being picked up and sent to Germany. She survived the war and expressed her gratitude many years after, when I visited Holland from Canada.

Although we had sufficient access to dairy products, we still lacked warm clothes during cold winters, foodstuffs other than dairy, footwear, and heating fuel. The whole family, except my father, who we thought deserved respect in his retirement, became mobilized to produce woolen sweaters, underwear, and socks. We turned to the past to see how wool was made, and Jan constructed two beautiful spinning wheels for Cato and Ali. My sisters visited sheep farmers in the Alblasserwaard to obtain the raw wool. A barter was made, as money had lost much of its pre-war value: the farmer would get half of the spun wool and my sisters kept the other half.

At home, it was like a factory. My sisters spun wool all day and my mother made woolen sweaters, socks, and underwear. I had a slight role in the process: I transported the wool between my sisters and the farmers once contact had been established. I also was a willing guinea pig to wear any wool product my mother made, regardless of its outcome or shape. Most of her products were excellent and suited the need, but my mother had some other ideas of her own. She thought the war could last many years, and I was young and undoubtedly would grow. The result was that I wore very baggy sweaters and underwear, which had room for many years of growth. I readily adapted and rolled up the long and flabby woolen undershirts at waist level under my shirt, baggy sweaters, or pants, whatever was suitable under the circumstances. The funny bulges at my waist did not bother me, except on one occasion.

In the summer, I stayed for a few weeks with my cousin Sye and his wife in Lisse. As Lisse was not far from the sea, Sye and I biked one day to the nearest beach. The beach was full of people sunbathing. Since there was little privacy, Sye and I undressed as quickly as possible. The next thing I knew, Sye was choking with laughter and rolling in the sand. I felt like all eyes were on me. After I took off my pants, my bulging undershirt unfolded and rolled down to my ankles right on the beach. I felt so embarrassed. The incident made a lasting impression on Sye, as he still talked about it when I met him many years later in Canada.

We adapted to the food situation (other than dairy) in various ways. In 1944, when there was a shortage of all sorts of commodities, we looked at every opportunity to provide for our needs. Cato and Ali traded spun wool and textiles for wheat with the farmers. The textiles were acquired from my brother Gijs. Textiles became scarcer as the war progressed. By 1944, Gijs had little left to sell, but he stored sufficient stock to barter for other commodities. Unfortunately, that abruptly came to an end, when late in 1944, lightning hit the roof of the house of a friendly nearby farmer who had stashed most of Gijs's textiles in his attic. The textiles were all burned. There was a much worse fate at that same farm that year. The Landwacht (Uniformed Dutch Nazi sympathizers) betrayed five people hiding from the Nazis who lived in a room inside a haystack. They were rounded up and shot.

My sisters were excellent barterers for wheat, and my mother baked delicious breads. Like with the milk, we brought loaves to neighbours in need, as my mother was a very generous woman. Later, baking bread became difficult when we were no longer allowed to use electricity. If caught using it, one would be severely punished. My mother used a gas stove for cooking instead. To overcome the problem, Jan set up a stationary bicycle in our attic. A small generator was attached to the bicycle and connected to car batteries. We all took turns riding the bicycle to create electricity. With our electricity, we lit carbide lamps. At the same time, Jan inserted a needle through a tiny hole in the house electricity meter located in a small box near the front door. The needle stopped the meter from running, while we used electricity to the fullest extent. The threat of punishment if we were caught did not deter us. The setup was partly a cover-up in case we were checked by a meter reader or the German Police. The German Police took over several houses on the adjacent block of our street. One day, Germans visited our house unexpectedly. We were able to pull out the needle before we opened the front door and fortunately, my mother was not baking bread at the time.

Jan worked as a mechanic for a car garage in Gorinchem. Most of the repair during the last years of the war was on German army trucks. There were not many privately owned vehicles left at that time. Jan used the opportunity to steal food from the trucks brought in for repair. He often brought home stolen food. But once, Jan was caught taking a large bag of peas from a German truck. He was pistol-whipped by the German who caught him in the act, and was imprisoned in the cellar of the municipal hall. We were very worried our house would be searched, because Jan was a member of the Dutch Resistance. He had stored weapons underneath the floor of our front room. The storage place was accessible through a sawed-out piece of the wooden floor, covered with a carpet with a sofa on top. Cato visited Jan's employer to discuss how to get Jan out of prison. Cato and the employer came up with a brilliant idea. The employer talked to the Germans in charge and convinced them that Jan was an excellent mechanic and that without him, many of the German trucks could not be repaired. Besides being a mechanic, the employer indicated that Jan was somewhat crazy and didn't understand the consequences of taking food from the trucks he repaired. Within three days Jan was released and was back to repairing German trucks in the garage, but he continued to take every opportunity to steal food from the Germans.

Bicycles were a precious commodity during the war, as there was little else for transportation for the Dutch population. During the last years of the occupation, the Germans confiscated bicycles from the Dutch, as they needed them, too.

At one time, I was walking through the city gate at the Arkelstraat (one of the two main entrances to the old city), when a German soldier confiscated a bicycle from a citizen. The owner grabbed the bicycle from the soldier's hands and dashed with his bicycle in hand up the earthen city wall. The soldier shouted at the man to stop and laid his automatic machine gun on the railing of a small bridge nearby for support. He fired several salvos at the desperate fleeing man. As I stood within ten steps from the soldier, I held my breath. There were only the two of us, the soldier and me, at the scene. Everyone else had ran away. I was too fascinated by the man's courage to think of leaving. Fortunately, the man was not hit by bullets as he wildly zigzagged on his bicycle. This is the only time in my life I witnessed a man risking his life for a bicycle. Of course, it was a foolish act, but I greatly admired the man for his courage.

Each member of our family, except my mother, had a bicycle. By the end of 1943, there was only one left in our household, because we had run out of tires or the Germans had confiscated several of them. I did not abandon my bicycle after the tires were gone, but continued to ride it without tires between school and home until the wheels collapsed.

Riding a tireless bicycle made a hell of a noise. One of the teachers at the Home Economics school near our house used me as a clock: when she heard me come home for lunch, she would stop giving lessons to have lunch, too. After the bike collapsed, Jan gave me another one with good tires, for which I was extremely grateful. After all, a boy without a bicycle feels lost in Holland.

Jan was a bike snatcher par excellence. His own was confiscated by the Germans and he was given a useless coupon in return. The coupon was a promissory note indicating that the owner would receive a bicycle after the war was over. Jan soon replaced his confiscated bicycle with another from the Germans. He used a clever strategy to steal them. He did this only in the vicinity of our church. He would watch a German soldier leave his bicycle outside a building near the church. If the conditions were right, he would steal the bicycle quickly and hide it in the vestibule of the church. No German would look for stolen bicycles in a church. Jan would leave the bicycle for a day or two, and after that he would calmly ride it home. My sisters, Jan, and I all had our bicycles replaced in this manner. We felt great that we got even with the Germans in such a just manner. Best of all was that we could ride again.

In the summer of 1944, I committed a blunder. I am not proud of the incident, but I tell the story, because it beautifully demonstrates the instant reaction and adaptation by my family to the situation.

At that time, the Home Economics School for girls had been taken over by the Germans for use as a field hospital. Massive and horrible German war casualties were brought to the hospital. Dutch women who dated German soldiers were employed there. Dating German soldiers was detested by the Dutch, and the women paid for it after the war. On one occasion, two of those women were walking down our street toward the hospital. I called out, "Traitors!" The women got upset and dragged me toward the hospital.

To make matters worse, my mother, who saw the incident from the window, ran out of the door and shouted, "You nasty women! Leave the boy alone!" The women cowered and immediately let me go. Not long after the incident, I was in our backyard, when Ali suddenly appeared on the balcony. She frantically waved to me to flee, because the Germans had come to the front door. I immediately knew what was coming, so I jumped over the back fence, ran across the field behind our home, and entered the alleys between other houses. I moved through backyards behind walls and vegetation, and crossed several roads until I reached a haystack at a farm. My heart pounded heavily from the effort. It was hours later when a friend who had seen me flee called out that it was safe to return home.

In the meantime, my family suffered the consequences of my name calling. When two Germans entered our home, they asked for the "boy." My family replied that I had fled and did they not know my whereabouts. The Germans threatened to take my father instead if I would not be home in half an hour. Then they left. Well, what to do? My sister Cato consulted a lawyer for advice. The lawyer told her that under no circumstances should the "boy" return home, as he could be severely beaten or killed.

My brother Jan contacted our neighbour next door who was a cement contractor. He had considerable influence with the Germans, as he helped them build their bunkers. He also spoke German fluently. Our neighbour came to our house immediately to wait the return of the Germans. He was a gentle man, but could not resist the temptation of doing business with and making money from the Germans. Only one German returned to our house to ask for the "boy" again. This was fortunate, as it was easier to handle one instead of two soldiers. With two, they would not let their guard down, as one checks the other.

My family told the soldier that I was just a little boy. The soldier asked for my age. My mother replied that I was ten (actually I was thirteen), and showed him a photo of me as a ten-year-old. Our neighbour asked the soldier to sit down and to make himself comfortable, and asked if he had a family of his own in Germany. The soldier put his hand in his pocket and pulled out a wallet with a photo of his wife and two young children. He shed some tears and said he had not seen them in a long time. The conversation went on for some time, after which the soldier stood up. He said he would not take the case any further, but warned my family that if the "boy" behaved badly again, there would be severe consequences. After that he left. My family expressed their gratitude to our neighbour. I returned home, expecting severe punishment from my family, but they were so relieved and happy, they forgot about it.

We had two different types of people who shared our home for eight months during the German occupation. I call them "guests," although they were not real guests in the literal sense of that word. One type were the people hiding from the Germans, who came first; and the other, a German tank crew, who came later.

The first person hiding from the Germans, who stayed with us for four months during the first half of 1944, was a heavyset, middle-aged man. He was a diver with the Dutch Navy. He was not a great joy to me. Although his wife lived in Gorinchem, we were told he was in hiding from the Germans, so his wife could not be told where he was. We soon found out that the woman who walked in the park next to our house each weekend and who wiped her eyes with a handkerchief was his wife.

The man was given my bedroom next to the park and I had to sleep in the attic. The attic was a dark place with a small loft window. At night, when I went upstairs, I sang loudly, because I was afraid of the dark and ghostly atmosphere. That scary feeling was made worse by the drying and rotting tobacco leaves hanging from the beams supporting the roof, which gave the place the appearance of a jungle. I stooped underneath the leaves and ran to my bed at the other end of the attic, where I dove under the blanket. That ghostly atmosphere left such an impression on me that many years later, when I visited my mother in Holland, I still sang loudly during a night visit to the old attic.

The tobacco leaves belonged to my father, who was the only smoker in the family. He had long run out of pipe tobacco and cigars, so he grew his own tobacco in our backyard. A lot of the leaves did not dry properly in the attic, but being an addict, he smoked them anyway. So did his cronies, mainly retired school principals and teachers, who sought my father's company partly for his tobacco. When they were at our place, the whole room was full of smoke and fungoid tobacco smell. I could hardly talk for several days after. I did not know then that I was allergic to tobacco smoke. I never blamed my father for smoking, as at that time he was not aware of the health consequences, of lung and stomach cancer, from which he died.

There was another reason I did not enjoy the company of our "guest." He spied and tattled on me. He had seen from his window upstairs that a girl kissed me in the park. I was not aware he had seen us, but he raised the topic at the dinner table. He told my family he had seen me with a girl. I felt uneasy, but tried to look as indifferent as I could while I ate my meal. He continued with the topic for some time to obtain further details, but I did not respond. Even my family remained silent. My unease changed to annoyance that he, as a guest, brought up the topic at the table. I broke the silence and the spell that he had cast when I asked him to pass the potatoes.

The man in hiding was a voracious eater, and he went through large helpings of potatoes. He became a serious burden on our food resources. His need for large quantities of food may have been the main reason he was lodging with us. It was also the main reason we asked the Resistance to find someone else to take care of him. Our wish was granted, and the burden lifted. Needless to say, I jumped for joy when I returned to my own bedroom.

The second "guest" stayed with us for two months during the fall of 1944. He was about twenty years old and hailed from Groningen, where his family owned a small aviation business. Jan got him a job at the garage where he worked. Unfortunately, the man had sticky fingers.

Jan had saved some money and kept it in a cigar box up in the attic. One Sunday, after we had all returned from church, Jan noticed some money was missing, but he did not know how much. So, Jan counted the bills and wrote down the serial numbers. The next Sunday after church more bills had disappeared, and now Jan knew exactly how many and which bills were missing.

Jan confronted the man. I was not present at the confrontation, but I understand it was quite a scene. Jan put the cigar box on the dining table and asked the fellow if he had seen the box before. Initially he denied it, but after some prodding he admitted to having seen the box before. Jan told him he was the only one who could have taken the money. Again, the man initially denied it, but later admitted he had taken some money. Jan asked him how much. The fellow mentioned a certain amount. Jan replied it was more than that. His adversary mentioned a bigger amount, but Jan replied that he had taken more. I understand this went on for some time, until the fellow broke down and admitted the full amount stolen. His family was contacted and the next morning he was picked up by his father, who apologized profusely. The fellow was perhaps not truly in need of a hiding place. His habits may have been a problem for his father's business.

One December night in 1944, a tremendous noise next to my bedroom woke me up with a jolt. The house was shaking with what seemed to be a growing roar of engines. There were German voices shouting, and trees and shrubs were crashing in the adjacent park. I carefully pushed aside the curtain and saw tanks being parked among the trees. The next morning, there were four tanks next to our house. They likely were parked there for cover from air attacks. Camouflage nets were draped over the tanks. The large Red Cross sign on the roof of the nearby field hospital may have provided extra protection from an aerial attack.

We were soon contacted by German officers who looked around our house. They wanted our back room, the main sitting and dining room, for the tank crew. The smaller front room (with Jan's weapons underneath), the small kitchen and all of upstairs were left to us. We were happy our whole house was not taken over. About eight soldiers used the back room. They slept in old armchairs and on mattresses on the floor for the next two months. The soldiers, mostly twenty-year-olds, were no burden to us. They went their own way and we ours. As we encountered them each day, we initially greeted them politely, and after some time, engaged them in conversation. This was a first for us.

We had never talked on our own accord to German soldiers before, because we hated everything they stood for. For example, if a soldier asked for directions, we pointed the wrong way. This was the attitude of most Dutch. When Germans marched through a street in Gorinchem and sang "We Will Sail Against England," most people turned their backs to the marching column or disappeared from the street. Boys sometimes would call out, "Splash, splash, splash" at the end of their marching song, suggesting they would drown before reaching England. I was somewhat more anti-German than most Dutch boys, the feelings instilled by my fiercely independent family. For instance, when a group of boys, including me, looked curiously at the tanks for the first time, a soldier offered candies. All the boys accepted them, except me. The soldier felt offended, and tried to force a candy into my mouth, but without success. But when he left, I stole candy from the tank.

After two weeks, we conversed with most of the tank crew who lived with us. They were bright, educated, and a cheerful bunch. They may have belonged to an elite group, although they definitely were not SS. We were not afraid of them. We joked, and even told them they would soon lose the war. They laughed about that too and replied, "So what? We'll go home." They asked me questions like, "Are there any girls around?"

At Christmas, they all sang carols until midnight. We listened quietly in the front room. Before, we had considered them to be an aberrant and a devious race of the human species. Now we realized they were not all highly disciplined and technically advanced monsters, but people with feelings, like us. At the beginning of February, they and their tanks suddenly disappeared. I understand they made a counterattack across the big rivers to the south where the Allied forces were. Less than half the crew and only two of the four tanks returned to the park. Some of the survivors had lost an arm or a leg. They did not return to our house. I asked one survivor I met on the street where the others were, but he avoided my question and looked dispirited. That was the first time I felt sorry for German soldiers.

I cannot help but compare the relationships we had with the two men in hiding and the tank crew. It is ironic that I only have unpleasant memories of the people our family tried to help and made extensive sacrifices for, while of the German tank crew, I have no bad memories at all. The feeling of hate for the German occupation and its absence for the tank crew, when they no longer behaved like the enemy, puzzled me for some time. The puzzle was resolved when I began to understand that the feeling of hate is only as strong as one allows it to be.

The Last Stretch

During the last four months of the occupation, our supply of food and other commodities dwindled considerably. Once or twice a week, I went to the Centrale Keuken (Central Kitchen) with a pail to obtain food in addition to what we received with food coupons and from other sources. Kitchen foods were mainly soup, mashed potatoes, and porridge. The soup and mashed potatoes contained beets, carrots, and turnips, and a little meat. The meat had a lot of fat, cartilage, hairy skin and bones. The porridge was occasionally burnt and lumpy. We once found a mouse in the soup, but as a whole, the food was not bad. My sisters, Jan, and I ate everything, but not the mouse. My parents were fussy. After seeing the food from the Central Kitchen, they did not eat any of it. The Kitchen food made us flatulent. Sometimes one of us would go off like a firecracker to the merriment of other family members. I liked going to the Central Kitchen, because there always was some entertainment. People standing in line for food to be discharged from large barrels joked about their contents and the pails they carried. Ordinary pails had become scarce, and many people came with toilet pails and bedpans. Once, during an aerial attack, everybody in the food line dove for cover while pails flew noisily all over the place. It took some time to sort them out.

    I did not go to school during the harsh winter of 1944–1945, known as the "Hunger Winter," as there was no fuel to heat the schools. We kept warm by cutting trees and digging willow stumps for heating. The stumps were from *grienden*, the Dutch word for fields of willows. The grienden were accessible, as it had been a very cold winter, and Jan and I skated to them over frozen ditches. The digging and cutting of roots was hard work. We transported the roots home on a sleigh. Burning of these stumps in our stove provided little heat and much smoke, but it was better than nothing. Gliding silently along with long strokes on skates through the scenic Dutch polder and winter landscape provided its own compensation. Hares dashed from their snow covers and Kestrels hovered in the blue sky above. On one occasion, we surprised an owl, who stared at us with its large eyes from its hiding place in a griend. Another time, we caught Coots, whose feet were frozen to the ice. Although they contained little meat, the Coots were a welcome treat at the dinner table.

We felt extremely sorry for the people in the big cities. They suffered severely from the cold, and many starved to death. People walked all the way from Rotterdam to our region and traded anything of value they possessed for a sack of potatoes. Sometimes there were long lines of people pushing handcarts on the road to Rotterdam. They looked terribly tired with their hollow cheeks and worn-out clothes and shoes through which their toes protruded. I pitied them and sometimes helped to push their carts for a long way while they limped along. But how can you help? There were so many of them. Only the massive airdrop by the Swedish Red Cross and the liberation of Holland would later end the despair of people in the big cities.

During the last half of April and the first days of May 1945, I sensed a change in attitude. People's mood became more buoyant as they expected to be liberated soon. The oncoming spring boosted that mood, with primulas blooming in gardens and Blackbirds singing from roofs and Chaffinches in trees. People from all walks of life gathered together. They conversed with great animation and excitement about the coming end of the war. Class boundaries had evaporated. The German occupation must have acted like a pressure cooker on all of them. Soon the lid was going to be lifted.

On the evening of May 4, sometime around eight o'clock, a door across the street flew wide open and a neighbour came out singing the Dutch national anthem. The Germans had agreed to surrender. People came out of their houses. They were overwhelmed with joy. The burden was lifted!

Memories of the Liberation of Gorinchem

On the evening of May 4, 1945, we heard the Germans had surrendered Holland. I was fourteen years old. The Germans who had operated a field hospital in the park next to our house had disappeared from our neighbourhood a few weeks earlier. The German "Green Police," who occupied several houses on our street, not far from us, were gone too, so people were unafraid to show their feelings. I felt a strong urge to express mine actively.

A friend and I dragged a flare to the park. It had been dropped by Allied planes, but had not flared. The flare was in a shape of a cylinder and contained compressed silver-gray magnesium powder, attached to a small parachute. We pulled straw from the roof of a little shed and placed the flare on top of the straw. We lit a match at the edge of the pile of straw and ran. There was an explosion of flames, and an outburst of bright light that lit up the neighbourhood and evening sky. Neighbours ran to the edge of the park and cheered.

I later heard that people living four kilometers away had seen the bright light. But they were not the only ones. Germans had seen it too, but since the light lasted for only ten minutes, they knew only its approximate location. As darkness fell, people returned to their homes. When German soldiers arrived on bicycles twenty minutes later, shouting and shooting, our street was empty.

At about ten o'clock the next morning, a vehicle stopped in front of our house. I later heard it was called a jeep. In the jeep were two men dressed in khaki uniforms. They had chubby cheeks, unlike the German soldiers, who generally had taut faces. One of them had a cigarette dangling from his lower lip. The other had a gun in his hand with a spiked bayonet. I opened the door and said hello. When they responded in funny Dutch, I looked at them in amazement. I had expected Canadians, but who were they? They told me they were Belgians from Flanders. They asked me, "Where is the Nieuwe Hoven?" I said, "You are right in it, but there is also a street by that name and it is one block over." They restarted their jeep, and off they went. That was my first introduction to the Allied forces.

Half an hour later, I followed the jeep's direction to the Nieuwe Hoven. There I came upon an amazing sight. Hundreds, no, perhaps thousands of German soldiers were lined up in a long column that filled the entire street from beginning to end, and way beyond. They must have been disarmed earlier, as none carried any weapons. They looked completely dispirited, exhausted, and utterly defeated.

In sharp contrast, there were a handful of Canadian soldiers in front of the column. They waddled in a droll and nonchalant manner holding guns with spiked bayonets. This handful of lightly armed Canadians held the giant German column at bay. If the Germans had wanted to, they could have finished the Canadians in a second, but fortunately, the Germans appeared to be in a total state of torpor.

Some citizens drew the attention of the Canadians to the bicycles some of the Germans were holding. The Canadians gestured to the Germans in front of the column to drop the bicycles to the side of the street. The Dutch swarmed over the bicycles. What a scene it was! Many citizens of Gorinchem had a bicycle again.

In my wanderings all over Gorinchem later that day, I only saw a few Canadians or other Allied soldiers, and they did not look well organized. Perhaps they were early birds, way in advance of the main force. I felt a strange kinship with these early birds, because they took great risks and showed no fear.

The jubilant mood continued the following days. Canadians, mostly from Quebec, took over the former German field hospital in the park next to our home. They often gave us Dutch boys rides in their armed carriers. Many Dutch women now dated Canadian soldiers. Even one of the women who had previously dated German soldiers and whom I had called "traitor" was now dating a Canadian. She probably escaped the round-up by the Dutch Underground, as she lived off the beaten track. Switching quickly to a Canadian soldier may have saved her the fate of other Dutch women who dated the Germans and who were publicly humiliated, or worse.

Boys in our neighbourhood traded in military commodities—chocolate bars and Players cigarettes. I collected a large number of Canadian helmets that the soldiers gave me. With a friend, I put together a German machine gun, parts of which a German soldier had thrown into the bushes just before surrender. I also collected Canadian hand grenades, which my family quickly got rid of. We had no fear of weapons and treated bullets as collector's items. Through my trades, I obtained a flare pistol with cartridges. It became an instant sensation! In the evenings, I would shoot flares of many different colours into the sky. Although my right shoulder hurt from the kickback, I kept firing the pistol as the thrill outweighed the pain. A friend living on the same street wrote to me after thirty-eight years that the only thing he envied me for at that time was my flare pistol.

Observing the momentous surrender of German soldiers in Gorinchem, I felt happy that the war was over and justice had been achieved, but I did not rejoice in their humiliation and misery. Sharing our home with the German tank crew had taught me that German soldiers were ordinary human beings, who treated my family decently. It was their Nazi leaders and government who had misled the soldiers to invade peaceful neighbouring countries, with devastating consequences. The German surrender gave the Dutch people hope that this was the beginning of a new Europe with lasting peace among its nations.

Photo on the front cover of Under Nazi Rule.
The Dutch in wartime, survivors remember.
(Photo and caption credit: Tom Bijvoet)
The War Memorial in Wilhelmina Park in Gorinchem commemorates the defiant and courageous stance of the civilian population during the occupation. A motherly figure stands erect in defiance of the foreign oppressor, one hand scrunched into a fist, the other resting protectively on her child's shoulder. A longing gaze of fear about and acceptance of the fate of her absent husband is directed toward the south from where freedom must come. A quote from the thirteenth stanza of the Dutch national anthem on the base of the statue reads: "Steadfast has remained my heart in adversity." The statue by Irma van Rappard-von Maubeuge was erected in 1951.

PART IV
Tributes to Kees and Rebecca A. Vermeer

Kees Vermeer

Joint Conference of the Colonial Waterbird Society and the Pacific Seabird Group, Victoria, British Columbia, November 8–12, 1995.

Immigrant Gone to Heaven

Colonial Waterbird Society - Pacific Seabird Group

CONTENTS	
Hotel Map	(inside front cover)
"Conference at a Glance"	1
Information for Contributors	2
Speakers	2
Badges	2
Banquet	3
Field Trips	3
"From the Organizers"	4
Program	5
Abstracts	29
Kees Vermeer: Scientist and Conservationist	95
Index	123

Our friend and colleague **Kees Vermeer** retired last year after three decades with the Canadian Wildlife Service. His career was devoted to the science and conservation of birds, and this section of the program is dedicated to him and his contribution.

Contents of the Joint Conference of the Colonial Waterbird Society and the Pacific Seabird Group— Kees Vermeer: Scientist and Conservationist.

Kees Vermeer: Scientist and Conservationist
Robert W. Butler

The Early Days

When Kees Vermeer set foot in British Columbia in April 1954, he must have thought he had died and gone to heaven. The vastness of unspoiled British Columbia was a freshness long forgotten in the postwar Netherlands. Kees had read about Canada, and was seeking new adventure after a tiring two-year spell in the Dutch army. He knew that British Columbia was the most scenic and mildest province in Canada, and set off across country by train to see it for himself.

Kees's interest in those early days was nature study, but he thought his best chances would be homesteading or farming. His first job was as a farmhand near Deroche and Chilliwack in the lower Fraser River Valley, east of Vancouver. At a monthly wage of only $80, Kees soon realized that he would never be able to afford a farm. He moved on to other seasonal jobs before landing a summer position in 1960 at the Pacific Biological Station at Nanaimo, studying orientation and navigation of salmon smolts.

British Columbia lies along the migration route between the immense breeding grounds in Alaska and western Canada, and winter quarters in the southern Western Hemisphere. Millions of loons, grebes, shorebirds, gulls, and waterfowl migrate along the coast each spring and autumn. Shorebirds and waterfowl are particularly numerous during migration and in winter in the protected waters of inlets and estuaries of British Columbia. Especially large concentrations are found in the Strait of

Georgia. Seabirds breed in large numbers on small islands northwest of Vancouver Island and the shores of the Queen Charlotte Islands. An estimated 5.6 million seabirds and 1.7 million waterfowl nest in the province. The province holds at one time of the year most of the world's American Black Oystercatchers, Marbled Murrelets, Cassin's Auklets, Rhinoceros Auklets, Western Grebes, Trumpeter Swans, Harlequin Ducks, Barrow's Goldeneyes, Surf Scoters, Glaucous-winged Gulls, Bald Eagles, and Western Sandpipers. Despite this abundance of birds, ornithology was still in its infancy in British Columbia in the 1960s. Brooks and Swarth (1925) and Munro and Cowan (1949) had completed pioneering work on bird distribution in the province, but ecological studies were few.

The Turning Point

There are moments in people's lives when a single event changes the course of their careers forever. For Kees, this moment came in the summer of 1960. A small group of students and professors at the University of British Columbia were pioneering research of coastal birds on Mandarte Island in southwestern British Columbia. Among them was Rudi Drent. He and Charlie Guiguet, at the BC Provincial Museum in Victoria, were compiling a catalogue of seabird nesting islands and they called upon Kees to census seabirds on Snake Island near the Pacific Biological Station in Nanaimo. The visit to the island was the turning point in Kees's career. He became deeply interested in the behaviour of nesting gulls, of which little was known. Kees approached Rudi Drent on studying gulls for a graduate degree and Rudi referred Kees to Dr. Miklos Udvardy, then professor at the University of British Columbia (UBC). The following year, Kees joined Frank Tompa on Mandarte Island where he began his classic study of the Glaucous-winged Gull (Vermeer 1963, Ydenberg, this publ.).

The Canadian Prairies

After completion of his Master of Science degree at UBC, Kees moved to the University of Alberta to complete his doctoral studies on the breeding ecology of Ring-billed Gulls and California Gulls under the supervision of Dave Boag. There he met and married Rebecca. Toward the end of his university studies in Alberta in 1966, Kees was offered a biologist position with the Canadian Wildlife Service (CWS) in Edmonton. His supervisors wanted him to survey waterfowl populations, but in characteristic inventiveness, he surveyed pelicans, herons, and cormorants in the Canadian prairies. He was given a truck, boat, and travel funds, and sent to explore the prairies, which was a dream come true for Kees. Many of these surveys stand today as the only population data for these species in the Canadian prairies.

While on the Prairies, Kees became concerned about the effects of contaminants when it was discovered that fish in some rivers carried high levels of mercury. He pointed the finger at the hospital in Edmonton as the pollution source, which created a political stir.

Return to the British Columbia Coast

In 1972, CWS opened an office on the Alaksen National Wildlife Area on the Fraser River delta, south of Vancouver. CWS had a long history of conducting seabird studies on the Atlantic Coast and Kees saw this as an opportunity to return to British Columbia to begin seabird studies on the Pacific Coast. He moved to the Institute of Ocean Sciences in Sidney, where he would remain for the rest of his career with CWS. While his colleagues in CWS were surveying waterfowl populations and assessing their habitats in the province, Kees began seaduck surveys along the coast and seabird surveys at sea (Vermeer and Rankin 1984a, 1985, Vermeer et al. 1983, Vermeer et al. 1987, Morgan et al. 1991). However, it was his long-time ambition to document the breeding biology of the seabirds of the northeast Pacific that captured his imagination.

With a small budget, Kees and his co-workers began studies on Triangle Island, a windswept, treeless island about forty kilometres northwest of Vancouver Island. He published over fifty-five papers with his co-workers on studies of the Rhinoceros Auklet, Tufted Puffin, Cassin's Auklet, Double-crested Cormorant, Pelagic Cormorant, Ancient Murrelet, Bonaparte's Gull, Mew Gull, Fork-tailed Storm-petrel, Leach's Storm-petrel, Pigeon Guillemot, and Black Oystercatcher. These were among the first studies of breeding seabirds in British Columbia.

Kees's earlier experience with contaminants and ducks in the Canadian prairies continued to attract his interest. He recognized the usefulness of birds as indicators of pollution (Vermeer 1971) and adapted this idea to studies of waterfowl in British Columbia (Vermeer and Peakall 1979). He also contributed information on the diet of ducks and seabirds on the British Columbia coast (e.g., Vermeer and Levings 1977, Vermeer 1981, 1982a, 1982b).

In the 1980s, other biologists began to work on seabirds in British Columbia. Over about five years, Michael Rodway and Moira Lemon completed a herculean task of estimating the numbers of nesting seabirds on most colonies on the British Columbia coast (Rodway 1988, Rodway 1991, Rodway et al. 1988, 1990). Meanwhile, Tony Gaston provided insight into the ecology and behaviour of the Ancient Murrelet in the Queen Charlotte Islands (Gaston 1992).

Research and Conservation

Although Kees's interest in conservation issues began early in his career with a proposal for a park in the Canadian Prairies, it was later in his career that conservation issues rose in prominence. The conferences and meetings he attended allowed him to collaborate with many colleagues on publications promoting the conservation of seabirds (e.g., Vermeer and Sealy 1984, Vermeer and Rankin 1984b, Vermeer et al. 1984). He also edited books on ecology and behaviour of gulls, estuaries, and ecosystems (Hand et al. 1987, Vermeer and Butler 1989, Vermeer et al. 1992, Vermeer et al. 1993, Butler and Vermeer 1994).

One of Kees Vermeer's greatest contribution to conservation was his ability to fill gaps in our knowledge on birds. Kees was among the first to publish on the nesting distribution and population status of herons, pelicans, and cormorants in the Canadian Prairies, eggshell thinning from pesticides (Vermeer and Reynolds 1970), metal pollution (Vermeer 1971, Vermeer and Peakall 1979), birds as indicators of pollution (Vermeer and Windsor 1971, Vermeer 1976), oil pollution effects on birds (Vermeer and Vermeer 1975), diet studies of waterfowl (Vermeer and Levings 1977), and the ecology of seabirds (over fifty papers, see Publication List in the Appendix).

Kees Vermeer understood early on that conservation required ecological studies and surveys of populations of all bird species. Kees's contribution to conservation will be remembered whenever one researches the field for information on seabird growth, diet, and distribution; sea duck distribution and diet; effects of mariculture, heavy metals, dioxins, and oil on waterbirds; numbers of waterbirds in estuaries; and distribution of eagles in British Columbia.

In recent years, others have shared Kees' views on conservation. His long time wish for the establishment of a field station on Triangle Island to study the demographics of seabirds on the British Columbia coast (Vermeer et al. 1992) was realized when Fred Cooke and Ian Jones installed a camp there in 1993.

In 1994, Kees retired from CWS where he is an Emeritus Scientist. His enthusiasm for bird study has not waned. The call of interior wetlands has led him to build a cabin on a remote Cariboo Lake where he can study birds at his leisure.

Literature Cited

Brooks, A.J. and H.S. Swarth. 1925. A distributional list of the birds of British Columbia. Avifauna Number 17, Cooper Ornithological Society, Berkeley, California.

Butler, R.W. and K. Vermeer (eds.). 1994. Abundance and distribution of birds in estuaries in the Strait of Georgia, British Columbia. Canadian Wildlife Service Occasional Paper Number 83, Ottawa.

Gaston, A.J. 1992. The Ancient Murrelet. T. and A.D. Poyser, London.

Hand, J.L., W.E. Southern and K. Vermeer (eds.). 1987. Ecology and behaviour of gulls. Studies in Avian Biology 10. 140pp.

Morgan, K.H., K. Vermeer and R.W. McKelvey. 1991. Atlas of pelagic birds of western Canada. Canadian Wildlife Service Occasional Paper Number 72, Ottawa.

Munro, J.A. and I. McTaggart Cowan. 1949. The bird fauna of British Columbia. Special Publication Number 2, British Columbia Provincial Museum, Victoria.

Rodway, M.S. 1988. British Columbia seabird inventory: report no. 3. Canadian Wildlife Service Technical Report Number 43, Canadian Wildlife Service, Delta, B.C.

Rodway, M.S. 1991. Status and conservation of breeding seabirds in British Columbia. Pp. 43–102 in J.P. Croxall (ed.). Seabird status and conservation: a supplement. ICBP Tech. Publication Number 11, Cambridge, UK.

Rodway, M.S., M. Lemon and G.W. Kaiser. 1988. Canadian Wildlife Service seabird inventory report no. 1: East coast of Moresby Island. Canadian Wildlife Service Technical Report Number 50, Canadian Wildlife Service, Delta, BC.

Rodway M.S., M. Lemon and G.W. Kaiser. 1990. Canadian Wildlife Service seabird inventory report no. 2: West coast of Moresby Island. Canadian Wildlife Service Technical Report Number 65, Canadian Wildlife Service, Delta, BC.

Vermeer, K. 1963. The breeding ecology of the Glaucous-winged Gull *Larus glaucescens* on Mandarte Island, B.C. British Columbia Museum Occasional Paper Number 13, Victoria.

Vermeer, K. and L.M. Reynolds. 1970. Organochlorine residues in aquatic birds in the Canadian Prairie Provinces. Canadian Field Naturalist 84:117–130.

Vermeer, K. 1971. A survey of mercury residues in aquatic bird eggs in the Canadian Prairie Provinces. Transactions of the North American Wildlife and Natural Resources Conference 36:138–152.

Vermeer, K. and J.A. Windsor. 1971. Spotted Sandpipers as possible indicators of mercury contamination of rivers. Blue Jay 29:59–60.

Vermeer, K. and R. Vermeer. 1975. Oil threat to birds on the Canadian west coast. Canadian Field Naturalist 89:278–298.

Vermeer, K.1976. Colonial auks and eiders as potential indicators of oil pollution.Marine Pollution Bulletin 9:165–167.

Vermeer, K. and C.D. Levings. 1977. Populations, biomass and food habits of ducks on the Fraser Delta tidal flats. Wildfowl 28:49–60.

Vermeer, K. and D.B. Peakall. 1979. Trace metals in sea ducks of the Fraser River Delta intertidal area. Marine Pollution Bulletin 10:189–193.

Vermeer, K. 1981. The importance of plankton to Cassin's Auklets during breeding. Journal of Plankton Research 3:315–329.

Vermeer, K. 1982a. Food and distribution of three *Bucephala* species in British Columbia waters. Wildfowl 33:22–30.

Vermeer, K. 1982b. Comparison of the diet of the Glaucous-winged Gull of the east and west coasts of Vancouver Island. Murrelet 63:80–85.

Vermeer, R and K. Vermeer. 1974. Oil pollution of birds: an abstracted bibliography. Pesticide Section. Canadian Wildlife Service Report 29:1–60.

Vermeer, K., I. Robertson, R.W. Campbell, G. Kaiser and M. Lemon.1983. Distribution and densities of marine birds on the Canadian west coast. Canadian Wildlife Service, Delta, BC.

Vermeer, K. and L. Rankin. 1984a. Pelagic seabird populations in Hecate Strait and Queen Charlotte Sound: comparison with the west coast of the Queen Charlotte Islands. Canada Technical Report, Hydrography and Ocean Sciences, Number 52, Sidney, BC.

Vermeer, K. and L. Rankin. 1984b. Influence of habitat destruction and disturbance on nesting seabirds. Pp. 723 -736 in J.P. Croxall, P.G.H. Evans and R. W. Schreiber (eds.). Status and conservation of the world's seabirds. ICBP Technical Publication Number 2, Cambridge, UK.

Vermeer, K. and L. Rankin. 1985. Pelagic seabird population in Dixon Entrance. Canada Technical Report, Hydrography and Ocean Sciences, Number 65, Sidney, BC.

Vermeer, K. and S.G. Sealy. 1984. Status of nesting seabirds of British Columbia. Pp.29–40 in J.P. Croxall, P.G.H. Evans and R.W. Schreiber (eds.) Status and conservation of the world's seabirds. ICBP Technical Publication Number 2, Cambridge, UK.

Vermeer, K., S.G. Sealy, M. Lemon and M. Rodway. 1984. Predation and potential environmental perturbances on Ancient Murrelets nesting in British Columbia. Pp. 757–770 in J.P. Croxall, P.G.H. Evans and R.W. Schreiber (eds.). Status and conservation of the world's seabirds. ICBP Technical Publication, Number 2, Cambridge, UK.

Vermeer, K., R. Hay and L. Rankin. 1987. Pelagic seabird populations off southwestern Vancouver Island. Canada Technical Report, Hydrography and Ocean Sciences, Number 87, Sidney, BC.

Vermeer, K. and R.W. Butler (eds.). 1989. The ecology and status of marine and shoreline birds of the Strait of Georgia, British Columbia. Canadian Wildlife Service Special Publication, Ottawa.

Vermeer, K., R.W. Butler and K.H. Morgan. (eds.). 1992. The ecology, status and conservation of marine and shoreline birds on the west coast of Vancouver Island. Canadian Wildlife Service Occasional Paper Number 75, Ottawa.

Vermeer, K., K.T. Briggs, K.H. Morgan and D. Siegel-Causey (eds.) 1993. The status, ecology and conservation of marine birds of the North Pacific. Canadian Wildlife Service Special Publication, Ottawa.

Edward Grey Institute of Field Ornithology

Botanic Garden
Oxford

30th October, 1963

Dear Vermeer,

You may remember that I met you on Mandarte Island one and a half years ago. I have just been looking at your thesis of which Dr. Tinbergen has a copy and which he lent to me and am naturally highly interested in your finding that the Gulls could raise families of four, five, and even six young successfully. Your results on this seem entirely convincing. However, I would be most grateful if you could clarify one point dealing with Table 25 on p. 74 of your thesis. Here you analyse the recoveries in relation to brood size at fledging. I think it would be more rewarding if you analyse these recoveries in relation to the brood size at hatching (including your supplemented broods of course). I cannot derive this from your Table since you merely group the young seen later according to the brood size when they left the nest. Since the mortality was similar for broods of all sizes, I have little doubt that the same result will ensue but I would greatly have liked to know whether this is in fact the case. Could you therefore have reconstructed Table 25 in terms of the original brood sizes?

To interpret your result and yet save my hypothesis of clutch size, I would think it possible that the gulls have at the present time an extremely abnormally favorable food situation, and that owing to their possession of three brood patches, they cannot quickly change their clutch size to meet a situation of this kind. Do you think this is a possible idea? Of the various other birds for which a similar test has been made lately, both the Laysan Albatross and Leach's Petrels seem to be unable to raise more than a single chick, but Gannets on the Bass Rock could raise two, though their clutches normally consist of one. The Gannets also are in an unusually favorable food situation at the present time, but we do not know to what extent the parents may have been strained to feed them.

Dr. Tinbergen was not sure where you are working now, but I am sending this letter to the UBC in the hope that it will be forwarded to you if you have now left there.

Yours sincerely,

David Lack

Early Days: Clutch Size Studies and the Thrill of Biological Discovery
Ron Ydenberg

Kees Vermeer published a single paper on clutch size very early in his career (Vermeer 1963). In fact, only a portion of the paper concerned clutch size; the rest was a general treatise on the breeding biology of the glaucous-winged gull (*Larus glaucescens*). But in spite of its status as a "mere" Master's thesis, that it was published in its entirety in an obscure provincial series (Occasional Papers of the British Columbia Provincial Museum), and that it moreover had the bad luck to be Number 13 in that series, Vermeer's monograph has been widely and frequently cited, especially in recent years. In 1989, it achieved the very real distinction of becoming a Citation Classic. All the more remarkable is that this was Vermeer's first published paper, being followed closely by a co-authored note published in The Condor (Vermeer et al. 1963), entitled "Aberrant Glaucous-winged Gulls." As we shall see, subsequent events added an ironic flavor to this title.

Students today (and probably then, too) would likely be astonished by the temerity of the then Master's student Vermeer. In his thesis, he challenged ideas of three of the biggest names in the field—Lack, Tinbergen, and Fraser Darling (not an unimpressive lineup). For example, both Lack's clutch size hypothesis and Fraser Darling's colony size-synchrony hypothesis were popular ideas at the time Vermeer was working, but were refuted by his data, and Vermeer said so in print. To top it all off, Kees turned down an offer to do a Ph.D. study (then a much rarer commodity than now) at Oxford with Niko Tinbergen, who later won a Nobel Prize, electing instead to go to the University of Alberta where he did a comparative study of the breeding biology of two inland-breeding gull species. Early in his career, Kees developed the habit of doing exactly what he pleased, being swayed neither by offers of fame nor by threats of discipline. In his native Dutch language Vermeer would have been called a *snotneus* (and probably was). I leave it to the imagination of readers not literate in Dutch to guess at the meaning of this endearing little word.

It was a time of debate about the biology of behaviour. For example, Tinbergen's 1953 book *The Study of Instinct* addressed the so-called "nature-nurture" controversy, and was still very influential. The year 1963 saw the publication of a major work promoting ideas very different from those of David Lack. V.C. Wynne-Edwards was a seabird biologist, and his book *Animal Dispersion in Relation to Social Behavior* has earned an important place in the history of evolutionary studies, because it for the first time made explicit use of group selection arguments to explain, among a whole variety of other behaviours, the small clutches of seabirds and other species. Wynne-Edwards's clear use of group selection logic quickly made its fallacy clear to a number of theorists, foremost among them George Williams, and revealed that many previous writers, including Tinbergen, often implicitly used such logic.

But in 1963 these issues were by no means settled, and Lack was very concerned about the implications of Vermeer's results for his hypothesis, a worry that he expressed in a letter written to Kees after Tinbergen loaned him a copy of the thesis. (His letter is reproduced at the start of this paper.) In it, Lack put forward an idea that soon formed the orthodoxy about the evolution of clutch size, adhered to by many investigators even though other studies showed the same results Vermeer had obtained. Lack suggested that food supply for Vermeer's gulls was extremely favourable, due to human activities in the form of garbage dumps and other refuse. He argued that because these anthropogenic influences were recent, gulls had not had time to evolve a greater clutch size. By extension, he reasoned that if the dumps were not there, gulls would be able to raise only three chicks. This libertine speculation was often used and promoted by subsequent investigators, so much so that contradictory data were ignored or erroneously reported as supporting Lack's hypothesis. For example, in a 1990 paper Schnaffer writes, "Based on results of numerous twinning studies demonstrating failure to raise two chicks, most authors agree that the one-egg clutch [of seabirds] is an adaptation to energy-limitation ... ."

Contrary to this and many other similar assertions, my survey with Doug Bertram (Ydenberg and Bertram 1989) of the brood enlargement literature in seabirds found that parents increased their fledging success in nineteen of twenty-five studies, and in fifteen of twenty-one species, including two of five procellariiforms. Very few of these authors were willing to conclude, as did Vermeer, that Lack was wrong. A notable exception was Brian Nelson, who carried out another large field experimental test of Lack's hypothesis, on Atlantic gannets, and published it in 1964, early enough to avoid the weight of opinion.

Ironically, Nelson's results have often been cited in support of Lack's post hoc modification to his hypothesis. By a curious logic, some investigators claimed that Lack's hypothesis predicts that gannets should be able to rear twins, because of the recent appearance of a new food source in the form of offal from fishing boats. A study of the southern gannet by Jarvis in 1973 was relevant and often cited, because here the offal was absent. Writers on the subject claimed that Jarvis's results supported Lack's idea, but this dubious assertion depends entirely on bad arithmetic. Jarvis's results actually show that southern gannets can rear enlarged broods. Ward repeated Vermeer's study a decade later in a large investigation (210 experimental broods) on Glaucous-winged Gulls in the Queen Charlotte Islands, a place chosen specifically for its lack of large garbage dumps. He repeated Vermeer's result, but now Lack argued that even in remote Haida Gwaii native egg hunting had so depressed the population that the food situation was abnormally favourable, and Ward never published his 1973 thesis. Was the Glaucous-winged Gull indeed an aberrant bird, as the title of Vermeer's second paper suggested?

Subsequent studies have shown that Vermeer and Ward were entirely correct in their conclusions about the ability of Glaucous-winged Gulls to rear clutches as large as six eggs. Moreover, garbage has been shown to be a poor food source, and individual gulls using natural foods perform better. Not a shred of evidence has emerged to support Lack's post hoc explanation of the results. Indeed, it has become widely accepted in the last ten years that the clutch that most species lay is smaller than the maximum that they could rear (the "Lack" clutch size). This finding has been extended to other situations than altricial bird species, such as parasitoid wasps. The question has become a classic puzzle for evolutionary ecologists, but the discipline might have begun solving this question twenty-five years earlier had they been more ready to accept Vermeer's results at face value and less concerned with defending Lack's idea.

Current clutch size research is using several main ideas to explain the discrepancy between observed and Lack clutch sizes. Different ideas or combinations of them are appropriate in different circumstances, but here is a brief summary. The *life history hypothesis* is that parents could enlarge their current effort to rear more offspring, but only at some cost such as physiological wear or the risk of depredation, with the effect of reducing the expected number of future offspring. The size of the present clutch is set by the trade-off between present and future reproduction, and is less than the maximum possible. Many studies claim to have documented such costs of reproduction.

The *geometrtc mean hypothesis* relies on the notion of an environment that varies unpredictably. Because of the geometric nature of population growth, a large clutch size that introduces annual variation in reproductive success (too optimistic in poor years, reducing the overall number of recruits, and high reproduction in good years) produces a lower long-term rate of increase than would a more conservative clutch size (lower but always reliable reproduction). The concept is analogous to that of high yield-high risk investments vs. blue chip stocks. In the long run the latter always earn more, which is why they are "blue chip." This notion has remained mostly in the theoretical realm.

The *individual optimization hypothesis* suggests that environments are predictable, and that parents can adjust the clutch size to match their individual circumstances. Clearly this does not apply to most seabirds (they lay clutches of fixed size, three in the case of most gulls) but a number of excellent studies on passerines shows that clutches enlarged or reduced from the size chosen by the parents produce fewer recruits. This arises because the offspring from enlarged clutches are less likely to survive;

reduced clutches produce "better" individuals, but fewer of them. Lack explicitly realized this trade-off, but its relevance here is that the largest clutches are the most successful because the clutch size optimum varies between individuals.

Another important aspect is the *lay date-clutch size trade-off*. It has been observed almost universally that earlier clutches are larger, and more successful. It is also known that later-born young are less likely to recruit, although the mechanism here is poorly understood. Hence, we can think of the parents as weighing up the continued accumulation of reserves so that a larger clutch can be laid, and the delay in clutch initiation required to accumulate the necessary nutriment. The solution to this trade-off is a continual decline in the optimum clutch size, so that most clutches will be smaller than the largest observed to be reared.

I mentioned above that Vermeer also tackled Fraser Darling's hypothesis, that one function of colonial nesting in birds such as gulls is to produce the mutual stimulation necessary to achieve breeding condition. With the hindsight afforded by forty years' experience with glib functional ideas, we can recognize this as one of the most glib. Today it seems inconceivable that naturalists should have overlooked the fact that many birds, even close relatives of the gulls, are solitary breeders not in need of "mutual stimulation," but such inconsistencies were far less obvious then than they are now, and it would be an historical arrogance to be too critical. The hypothesis was very popular, and did at least have the virtue of a clear quantitative prediction: that large colonies breed more synchronously than small colonies. It attracted a lot of attention, and Vermeer tested the synchrony prediction. In typical fashion, he expends little ink on a discussion of the issues, instead reporting the data, and summarizing simply (p. 91) that "No support was found for the Fraser Darling effect … ."

I would like to mention one further contribution of Kees's that bears on Lack's ideas about energy limitation in seabirds. Many investigators were bothered by details of the twinning experiments. In particular, many felt that the manipulation created an "abnormal" situation, either because the parents could not brood two chicks, or because doubled demand was too great an increment, or because having two nestlings was too unusual. The strength of these objections was largely eliminated as a result of an elegant experiment with two tropical pelagic-feeding terns. Shea and Ricklefs (1985) fostered nestlings of the large sooty tern (*Sterna fuscata*; 175 g) into the nests of a smaller species, the gray-backed tern (*Sterna lunata*; 150 g), and found that gray-backed tern parents increased their provisioning by 25 percent, relative to control parents raising their own offspring, and maintained the higher level of work for a full month. These results indicate that parent terns normally work at a level below the maximum, and that they are able to increase the rate of provisioning under at least some circumstances. Vermeer actually carried out and published a similar experiment in 1979 (Vermeer and Cullen 1979, Ardea 67), using the same cross-fostering experimental design on rhinoceros auklets (*Cerorhinca monocerata*; 520 g) and tufted puffins (*Lunda cirrhata*; 745 g). The results matched those of Ricklefs, but the sample was smaller, the measures taken less extensive, and little discussion was given in the paper to these issues.

I believe Lack's clutch size hypothesis was so vigorously defended because it offered the strongest alternative to Wynne-Edwards's group selected reproductive restraint hypothesis, which, once it was clearly outlined, was quickly recognized by many scientists as untenable. It was the "lack" of other ideas as good as Lack's that could have helped accommodate observations of clutches smaller than the "Lack optimum" within an individual selection framework that created a dilemma for results like Vermeer's. Given this historical context, it is a plume in the hat of scientific process that it was cited as much as it was.

Looking at 1963 from the 1990s is much easier than the reverse. The three decades of perspective, and the luxury of a much better understanding of evolutionary studies permits one to attempt to sort the complicated historical cacophony of ideas and allegiances, of claims and counterclaims, of data and belief. Kees wisely avoided much forecasting in his 1963 paper, but in the note he wrote for the October 23, 1989 issue of Current Contents (reprinted below) that recognized his paper as a *Citation Classic*, he indulges in some historical speculation, suggesting that it was cited so often perhaps because it challenged Lack's hypothesis. The background of hot debate against which the monograph was published certainly made it timely, but I think that Kees is a bit too modest. His paper stands not only as the *first* experimental test of an idea that we now credit as very important in the development of evolutionary ecology, it is also one of the very *best*. Both the techniques that he developed and the sample sizes that he attained were often emulated, but rarely matched in similar studies even up to the present day. As such its value is enduring.

Reprinted from Current Contents, October 23, 1989

THIS WEEK'S CITATION CLASSIC
CC/NUMBER 43 OCTOBER 23, 1989

Vermeer, K. The breeding ecology of the Glaucous-winged Gull (Larus glaucescens) on Mandarte Island, B.C. (Whole issue).
Occas. Pap. Br. Columbia Prov. Mus. (13), 1963. 104p.

The breeding cycle of Glaucous-winged Gulls was investigated for a total of eight months in the summers of 1961 and 1962 on Mandarte Island, a small rocky island in the southern Strait of Georgia, British Columbia. The results of the major experiment of that study challenged the interpretation that the upper limits of the clutch of three eggs in gulls was set by the food requirements of the young. (The Science Citation Index indicates that this paper has been cited in over 100 publications, making it one of the most-cited papers in that series.)

Nesting Biology of
Glaucous-winged Gulls

Kees Vermeer
Canadian Wildlife Service
c/o Institute of Ocean Sciences
P.O. Box 6000
Sidney, British Columbia V8L 482
Canada

July 4, 1989

My interest in studying gulls began on a weekend in May 1960, when as a student assistant involved with fish orientation studies at the Pacific Biological Station in Nanaimo, I accompanied my supervisor on a field trip to photograph Glaucous-winged Gulls on a small rocky islet. This was the first time I had seen nesting gulls, and I became so intrigued with their behaviour that, from that moment on, I made up my mind to study gulls.

My previous plans to research some aspect of fish ecology for a master's degree evaporated and consequently so did my prospects of becoming employed in the field of fisheries. During the next two years, I conducted field investigations on Mandarte Island for a master of science degree at the University of British Columbia. On one occasion, my supervisor, Dr. Miklos Udvardy, brought David Lack, perhaps the most prominent avian ecologist living at that time, to the island. We had an enjoyable time discussing world events and birds, but only once was the subject of my study briefly brought up. I mentioned that I had added gull chicks to existing nests to create supernormal broods of four, five, and six chicks (the normal being three chicks or fewer) to determine if parents could raise extra-large broods. Lack predicted that the gulls would be unable to do so. I replied that if that were indeed true, it would support his hypothesis that the clutch size of each species of bird had been adapted by natural selection to correspond to the largest number of young for which the parents can, on average, provide enough food. At the end of that season I found (to my surprise as well) that parent birds were not only able to raise broods of four, but also of five and six chicks to the age of flight. Lack was very concerned about those results. Lack's clutch size hypothesis has triumphed so far, in spite of the outcome of many experimental studies that did not support the hypothesis. However, the last word on this theory may not yet have been said.

I do not know exactly why my first paper has been cited so frequently. Perhaps it was the challenge to Lack's hypothesis and/or the detailed documentation of other findings, some of which did not support statements made by other noted scientists in the field, such as Fraser Darling or Nico Tinbergen. Dr. Tinbergen, a Nobel Prize recipient, invited me to study under him in Oxford shortly after the completion of my study, an offer that I declined for pragmatic reasons. Whatever the reason(s) for this paper's success, I enjoyed my study immensely. Since then, I have been involved with many other studies of waterbirds and my enthusiasm for research remains unabated. But I will never forget the first thrill of biological discovery on Mandarte Island.

Kees Vermeer

Threats and Realities of Oil Pollution
The Research Contributions of Kees and Rebecca A. Vermeer
Alan E. Burger

The Torrey Canyon disaster off Cornwall, England, in 1967 caused a significant change in the assessment of oil spill risks throughout most of the world. More than thirty thousand seabirds were killed in that spill (Bourne 1970a,b), and for the first time, television audiences were exposed to the horror of a major spill. This, plus the proliferation of supertankers and offshore oil exploration, stimulated oil spill research in several countries in the following decade, e.g., Britain (Bourne 1968, 1970b, RUROS 1972, 1974), and the Netherlands (Swennen 1977, Swennen and Spaans 1970). In Canada, there had been sporadic reports on the effects of oil on seabirds (e.g., Horwood 1959), but no systematic reviews or research. At the same time, increasing tanker traffic and plans for offshore oil exploration were creating a demand for information on oil risks in Canada.

In the early 1970s, while working mainly on waterfowl and the effects of pesticides, Kees Vermeer recruited his wife Rebecca, and together they collected and reviewed a mass of published and unpublished literature on oil spills and the effects of oiling. This resulted in the publication in 1974 of two annotated bibliographies, on the impacts of oil on birds (Vermeer and Vermeer 1974a), and other aquatic organisms (Vermeer and Vermeer 1974b). These were thorough, ground-breaking compilations, which are still used extensively by researchers in these fields in Canada and many other parts of the world. One valuable feature was the inclusion of a large selection of unpublished "grey literature" in the form of government or consultant's reports, which are often overlooked and difficult to access. The oil-seabird bibliography was updated in 1987 by Kees and others (Hooper et al. 1987), and continues to be of international significance as the most complete bibliography of its kind.

Using their bibliography as a springboard, Kees and Rebecca published an influential paper on the threats from oil to seabirds on the Canadian west coast (Vermeer and Vermeer 1975). This paper was remarkable in the thoroughness of the literature review, the scope of topics covered, and the impacts it had on other work done in British Columbia and elsewhere. For example, the paper included a detailed review of most of the major tanker spills that had occurred in the world. Kees and Rebecca made it clear that the number of birds killed in an oil spill was not directly correlated with the volume of oil spilled, but was strongly affected by oceanographic conditions and the distributions and densities of birds. This was confirmed by later analyses (National Research Council 1985, Burger 1993a). The Vermeers' paper also pointed out that beach counts provided only a minimum count of bird mortality following a spill; many birds were lost at sea or disappeared off beaches. In the 1980s and 1990s, this problem was addressed through the development of complex probability models and experimental tests of rates of sinking and scavenging of carcasses, which have been used to assess the impacts of several recent spills (Ford et al. 1987, 1991, Burger 1993b, Ecological Consulting Inc. 1991).

Another feature was the Vermeers' review of the volumes and routes of shipping in BC to demonstrate where the risks of spills were greatest. In particular, they highlighted the risks of spillage from the increasing vessel traffic in the nearshore waters in BC, from tanker traffic carrying Alaska crude into Puget Sound, and from the oil loading facility at Cherry Point, Washington, near Boundary Bay. All of these risks exist today, with even greater volumes of shipping and oil transportation. In the 1990s, more than three hundred large tankers pass through the Strait of Juan de Fuca carrying Alaska crude. Cohen and Aylesworth (1990) analysed shipping movements and ocean conditions in a model which predicted that southern BC and northern Washington would be exposed to spills exceeding one thousand barrels every 1.3 years, and larger spills every four to five years. Spills of five thousand barrels or larger have, in fact, occurred in these waters at average intervals of 3.4 years (Burger 1992), confirming the dangers discussed in the Vermeer and Vermeer (1975) paper twenty years earlier.

The Vermeer and Vermeer (1975) review also demonstrated the need for information on bird densities, seasonal movements, and diets in order to assess risks of oil pollution. They identified the Fraser Delta/Boundary Bay region as an area of high risk, being a few kilometres away from the Cherry Point loading facility and supporting huge densities of waterfowl, shorebirds, and seabirds. This provided additional impetus for the ongoing monitoring and study of these important populations (e.g., Butler 1992, Butler and Campbell 1987). Another area identified as critical was the continental shelf sea off southwestern Vancouver Island, where there are high densities of birds, and high risks of oil pollution. Work undertaken by Kees and his co-workers confirmed the importance of this area for pelagic birds in all seasons (Vermeer et al. 1983, 1987, 1989, Morgan et al. 1991), and it is one of the few pelagic areas in BC in which systematic seabird surveys have been made. Kees's work off the west coast of Vancouver Island proved to be extremely important following the Nestucca oil spill in 1988, which affected much of the nearshore area of Vancouver Island, and killed an estimated fifty-six thousand seabirds (Ford et al. 1991). Comparison of Kees's aerial and shipboard census data with the species composition and distribution of oiled birds was a key component of the post-spill assessment (Rodway et al. 1989, Burger 1993b). Using the incomplete colony inventory available at the time, Vermeer and Vermeer (1975) also delineated critical areas in BC where breeding seabirds would be at greatest risk to oil pollution, such as the Scott Islands (including Triangle Island). The risks of oiling are often cited today as a key factor in promoting research in these critical areas.

Kees and Rebecca Vermeer (1975) were among the first to recognize that chronic small-scale spills were often equally or more damaging to seabird populations than the well-publicized catastrophic spills. They documented small spills in BC to highlight this problem. A decade later, Environment Canada records showed 574 spills reported annually in

BC, with hundreds of small spills not being reported (Kay 1989a,b). The effects of chronic small spills on seabirds in BC remain largely unknown, although at least 6 percent of all dead seabirds found on beached bird surveys were oiled, and oiling was the most common cause of death identified on exposed shores (Burger 1993c).

Another pattern which emerged from their reviews (Vermeer and Vermeer 1975, Vermeer and Anweiler 1975) was the susceptibility for oiling by diving birds, particularly alcids and diving ducks. This was further highlighted by Kees (Vermeer 1976), who went on to suggest that monitoring of alcid and sea duck populations would be an effective means of tracking the effects of oiling and other pollution. Murres and eiders were suggested as indicator species. Since this paper, changes in breeding populations of alcids, particularly murres, have been used to assess the effects of several spills, but there have been many disagreements over the interpretation of changes, and the precision of census needed to demonstrate significant changes (e.g., Boersma et al. in press, Parrish and Boersma 1995, Piatt and Anderson in press). It appears to be difficult to separate changes in populations caused by oil spills from those caused by other human causes (e.g., over-fishing or gill-netting) and natural phenomena (e.g., changes in local productivity).

Kees was one of the first biologists to point out the risks to Arctic populations of waterfowl and other birds from oil exploration in the Beaufort Sea (Vermeer and Anweiler 1975). This assessment was based on a combination of field surveys and reference to studies of spills in similar habitats where thousands of sea ducks and other birds had been killed. The study was among the first of many to investigate populations of birds on the shores of the western Arctic, and so contributed greatly to our understanding of this remote area.

Today, largely as a result of the Exxon Valdez, Nestucca, and Apex Houston oil spills, research on the impacts of oil spills and methods of restoration is big business, and unfortunately tainted by the aggression and intolerance of litigation lawyers. The contributions made by Kees and Rebecca Vermeer and their co-workers remain as landmark references. They have been keys to our appreciation of the risks of oil pollution in Canada and the rest of the world, and have greatly assisted and stimulated later research. In particular, they showed that a wide range of information was required to accurately assess the risks of oiling to seabirds. This includes information on shipping, oceanography, distribution of colonies, foraging and staging areas, diets, and the foraging areas of birds. Despite considerable work done in the past two decades, we remain ignorant of many aspects of these topics and their interrelationships.

Literature Cited

Boersma, P.D., J.K. Parrish, and A.B. Kettle. In press. Common Murre abundance, phenology, and productivity on the Barren Islands, Alaska: the Exxon Valdez oil spill and long-term environmental change. In Exxon Valdez oil spill: fate and effects in Alaskan waters (P.G. Wells, J.N. Butler and J.S. Hughes, eds.). ASTM Special Tech. Publ. No. 1219, American Society for Testing and Materials, Philadelphia, PA.

Bourne, W.R.P. 1968. Oil pollution and bird populations. Pp. 99–121 in The biological effects of oil pollution on littoral communities (J.D. Carthy and D.R Arthur, eds.). *Field Studies 2 (Suppl.)*.

Bourne, W.R.P. 1970a. Special review—after the 'Torrey Canyon' disaster. Ibis 112:120–125.

Bourne, W.R.P. 1970b. Oil pollution and bird conservation. Biol. Conserv. 2:300–302.

Burger, A.E. 1992. The effects of oil pollution on seabirds off the west coast of Vancouver Island. Pp. 120–128 in The ecology, status and conservation of marine and shoreline birds on the west coast of Vancouver Island (Vermeer K., R.W. Butler and K. Morgan, eds.). Canadian Wildlife Service Occ. Pap. No. 75, Ottawa.

Burger, A. E. 1993a. Estimating the mortality of seabirds following oil spills: effects of spill volume. Mar. Pollut. Bull. 25:140–143.

Burger, A.E. 1993b. Effects of the Nestucca oil spill on seabirds along the coast of Vancouver Island in 1989. Can Wildl. Serv. Tech. Rep. Ser. 179. 51p.

Burger, A.E. 1993c. Mortality of seabirds assessed from beached bird surveys in British Columbia. Can. Field-Naturalist 107:164–176.

Butler, R.W. (ed.) 1992. Abundance, distribution and conservation of birds in the vicinity of Boundary Bay, British Columbia. Tech. Rep. Series No. 155.Can. Wildl. Serv., Pacific and Yukon Region, British Columbia.

Butler, R.W. and R. W. Campbell. 1987. The birds of the Fraser River delta: populations, ecology and international significance. Can. Wildl. Serv. Occ. Pap., No. 65, Ottawa. 73 p.

Cohen, P. and R. Aylesworth. 1990. Oil spill risk for southern BC/ northern Washington coast marine area. Final report of the States/ British Columbia oil spill task force, Appendix VII. Publ. Province of British Columbia and the States of Washington, Oregon, Alaska and California. 105 p.

Ecological Consulting, Inc. 1991. Assessment of direct seabird mortality in Prince William Sound and the western Gulf of Alaska resulting from the Exxon Valdez oil spill. Unpubl. report Ecological Consulting Inc., Portland, Oregon.

Ford, R.G., G.W. Page and H. R. Carter. 1987. Estimating mortality of seabirds from oil spills. Pp. 747–751, in Proc. 1987 Oil Spill Conference, American Petroleum Institute, Washington, D.C.

Ford, R.G., J.L, Casey, C.H. Hewitt, D.B. Lewis, D.H. Varoujean, D.R. Warrick and W.A. Williams. 1991. Seabird mortality resulting from the Nestucca oil spill incident, winter 1988–89. Report for Washington Dept. Wildlife. Ecological Consulting Inc., Portland, Oregon.

Hooper, T.D., K. Vermeer and I. Szabo. 1987. Oil pollution of birds: an annotated bibliography. Can Wildl. Serv. Tech.Rep. Ser. 34. 180 pp.

Horwood, H. 1959. Death has a rainbow hue. Canadian Audubon 21:69–73.

Kay, B.H. 1989a. Pollutants in British Columbia's marine environment: a status report. Environment Canada, Conservation and Protection, SOE Report No. 89-1, Vancouver, B.C.

Kay, B.H. 1989b. Pollutants in British Columbia's marine environment. Environment Canada, Conservation and Protection, SOE Fact Sheet No. 89-2, Vancouver, B.C.

Morgan, K.H., K. Vermeer and R.W. McKelvey. 1991. Atlas of pelagic birds of Western Canada. Occ. Pap. 72, Can. Wildl. Serv., Ottawa.

National Research Council. 1985. Oil in the sea: inputs, fates and effects. National Academy Press, Washington, D.C.

Parrish, J.K. and P.D. Boersma. 1995. Muddy waters. Amer. Sci. 83:112–115.

Piatt, J.F. and P. Anderson. In press. Responses of Common Murres to the Exxon Valdez oil spill and long-term changes in the Gulf of Alaska marine ecosystem. In Oil spill symposium proceedings (S.D. Rice, R.B. Spies, D.A. Wolfe and B.A. Wright, eds). American Fisheries Society Symposium No. 18.

Rodway, M. S., J. F. Lemon, J.-P. Savard and R. McKelvey. 1989. Nestucca oil spill: impact assessment on avian populations and habitat. Tech. Rep. Ser. No. 68. Canadian Wildlife Service, Pacific and Yukon Region, British Columbia.

RUROS (Research unit on the rehabilitation of oiled seabirds). 1972. Third annual report of the advisory committee on oil research of the sea. Univ. Newcastle upon Tyne, U.K.

RUROS (Research unit on the rehabilitation of oiled seabirds). 1974. Fifth annual report of the advisory committee on oil research of the sea. Univ. Newcastle upon Tyne, U.K.

Swennen, C. 1977. Laboratory research on seabirds. Netherlands Institute Sea Research, Texel, Netherlands.

Swennen C. and A.L. Spaans.1970. De sterfte van zeevogels door olie in februari 1969 in het Waddengebied (Seabird mortality by oil in the Wadden Sea area in February 1969). Het Vogeljaar 18:233–245.

Vermeer, K. 1976. Colonial auks and eiders as potential indicators of oil pollution. Marine Poll. Bull. 9:165–167.

Vermeer, K. and G. Anweiler. 1975. Oil threat to aquatic birds along the Yukon coast. Wilson Bull. 87:467–480.

Vermeer, R. and K. Vermeer. 1974a. Oil pollution and birds: an abstracted bibliography. Pesticide Section. Can. Wildl. Serv. Rept. 29:1–60.

Vermeer, R and K. Vermeer. 1974b. Biological effects of oil pollution on aquatic organisms: a summarized bibliography. Pesticide Section. Can. Wildl. Serv. Rept. 30:1–68.

Vermeer, K. and R Vermeer. 1975. Oil threat to birds on the Canadian West Coast. Can. Field. Nat. 89:278–298.

Vermeer, K., K.H. Morgan, G.E.I. Smith and R Hay. 1989. Fall distribution of pelagic birds over the shelf off SW Vancouver Island. Colonial Waterbirds 12:207–214.

Vermeer, K.,I. Robertson, R. W. Campbell, R. W. Kaiser and M. Lemon. 1983. Distribution and densities of marine birds on the Canadian west coast. Can. Wildl. Serv. Rept., Vancouver, B. C.

Vermeer, K., R. Hay and L. Rankin. 1987. Pelagic seabird populations off southwestern Vancouver Island. Can. Tech. Rep. Hydrog. Ocean Sci. No. 87.

Publications by Kees Vermeer 1963–1994

This list of publications is part of the tributes published in the 1995 conference in Victoria, and was referred to by Robert Butler to demonstrate the scope of research undertaken by the author.

Vermeer, K. 1963. The breeding ecology of the Glaucous-winged Gull, *Larus glaucescens*, on Mandarte Island, B.C. Occ. Pap. Brit. Col. Prov. Mus. No.13 104pp. (Published M.Sc Thesis).

Vermeer, K., R.F. Oldaker, M.D.F. Udvardy and K. Kelleher. 1963. Aberrant Glaucous-winged Gulls. *Condor* 65:332–333.

Drent, R.H., G.F., VanTets, F. Tompa and **K. Vermeer**. 1964. The breeding birds of Mandarte Island, British Columbia. *Can. Field Nat.* 78:208–263.

Vermeer, K. 1967. Foreign eggs in nests of California Gulls. *Wilson Bull.* 79:341.

Vermeer, K. 1967. Common Terns nesting at Miquelon Lake, Alberta. *Can. Field Nat.* 81:274–275.

Vermeer, K. 1968. Ecological aspects of ducks nesting in high densities among larids. *Wilson Bull.* 89:78–83.

Vermeer, K. and B. Switzer. 1968. Road kills of birds and mammals in southeastern Alberta. *Blue Jay* 26:93–94.

Vermeer, K. 1969. Great Blue Heron colonies in Alberta. *Can. Field Nat.* 83:237–242.

Vermeer, K. 1969. Colonies of Double-crested Cormorants and White Pelicans in Alberta. *Can. Field Nat.* 83:36–39.

Vermeer, K. 1969. The present status of Double-crested Cormorant colonies in Manitoba. *Blue Jay* 27:72–73.

Vermeer, K. 1969. Some aspects of the breeding of the White-winged Scoter at Miquelon Lake, Alberta. *Blue Jay* 27:72–73.

Vermeer, K. 1969. Comparison of the helminth fauna of California Gulls, *Larus californicus* and Ring-billed Gulls, *Larus delawarensis* at Beaverhill and Miquelon Lakes. *Can. J. Zool.* 47:267–270.

Vermeer, K. 1969. Endoparasitic variation between California Gulls and Ring-billed Gulls, *Larus californicus* and *L. delawarensis*. *Ibis* 111:393–395.

Vermeer, K. 1969. Egg measurements of California and Ring-billed Gull eggs at Miquelon Lake, Alberta in 1965. *Wilson Bull.* 81:102–103.

Vermeer, K. 1969. Some aspects of the breeding chronology of Double-crested Cormorants at Lake Newell, Alberta in 1969. *Murrelet* 59:19–20.

Vermeer, K. 1970a. Breeding biology of California and Ring-billed gulls; a study of ecological adaptation to the inland habitat. *Can. Wildl. Rep.* Ser. No. 12. 52pp. (Published Ph.D. Thesis).

Vermeer, K. 1970b. Some aspects of the nesting of Double-crested Cormorants at Cypress Lake, Saskatchewan in 1969: A plea for protection. *Blue Jay* 28:11–13.

Vermeer, K. 1970c. Colonies of Double-crested Cormorants and White Pelicans in Saskatchewan. *Can. Field Nat.* 84:39–42.

Vermeer, K. 1970. Aquatic park proposal for Lake Winnipegosis, Kawinaw and Pelican Lakes. *Blue Jay* 28:66–67.

Vermeer, K. 1970. Insular Great Blue Heron colonies on large Manitoba lakes. *Blue Jay* 28:84–86.

Vermeer, K. 1970. Autumn migration of juvenile White Pelicans from western Canada. *Blue Jay* 28:88.

Vermeer, K. and G.C. Anweiler. 1970. Great Blue Heron colonies in Saskatchewan in 1970. *Blue Jay* 28:158–161.

Vermeer, K. 1970. Aquatic breeding birds of the Isle of Bays. *Blue Jay* 8:86–87.

Vermeer, K. 1970. A study of Canada Geese, *Branta canadensis*, nesting on islands in southeastern Alberta. *Can. J. Zool.* 43:235–240.

Vermeer, K. and L.M. Reynolds. 1970. Organochlorine residues in aquatic birds in the Canadian Prairie Provinces. *Can. Field Nat.* 84:117–130.

Vermeer, K. 1970. Breeding records of Herring Gulls in Alberta and California Gulls in Manitoba. *Can. Field Nat.* 84:102.

Vermeer, K. 1970. Large colonies of Caspian Terns on Lake Winnipeg and Lake Winnipegosis. *Blue Jay* 28:117–118.

Vermeer, K. 1970. Distribution and size of White Pelican colonies in Canada. *Can. J. Zool.* 48:1029–1032.

Vermeer, K. 1970. Arrival and clutch initiation of Double-crested Cormorants at Lake Newell, Alberta. *Blue Jay* 28:124–125.

Vermeer, K. 1971. A survey of mercury residues in aquatic bird eggs in the Canadian Prairie provinces. *Trans. N. Am. Wildl. And Nat. Resources Conf.* 36:138–152.

Vermeer, K. 1971. Some aspects of the breeding of Herring Gulls at Kawinaw Lake, Manitoba. *Blue Jay* 29:207–208.

Vermeer, K. and J.A. Windsor. 1971, Spotted Sandpipers as possible indicators of mercury contamination of rivers. *Blue Jay* 29:59–60.

Vermeer, K. 1971. The Pelican—Protection or Extinction. *Canadian Audubon* 33(4 and 5):103–104.

Vermeer, K. 1971. Large American Avocet clutches at Dowling Lake, Alberta. *Blue Jay* 29:83.

Vermeer, K. 1972. The crayfish, *Orconectes virilis,* as an indicator of mercury contamination. *Can. Field Nat.* 85:123–125.

Vermeer, K., D.R.M. Hatch and J.A. Windsor. 1972. Greater Scaup is common breeder on northern Lake Winnipeg. *Can. Field Nat.* 86:168.

Vermeer, K. 1972. Variation in density of breeding ducks across the aspen parklands and grasslands of Canada. *Blue Jay* 30:154–158.

Vermeer, K. and R.W. Risebrough. 1972. Additional information on eggshell thickness in relation to DDE concentrations in Great Blue Heron eggs. *Can. Field Nat.* 86:384–385.

Vermeer, K. and D.R.M. Hatch. 1972. Additional information on Great Blue Heron colonies in Manitoba. *Blue Jay* 30:89–92.

Vermeer, K. and F.A.J. Armstrong. 1972. Correlation between mercury in wings and breast muscles in ducks. *J. Wildl. Mgmt.* 36:1270–1273.

Vermeer, K. and F.A.J. Armstrong. 1972. Mercury in Canadian prairie ducks. *J. Wildl. Mgmt.* 35:179–182.

Vermeer, K. 1972. Comparison of the clutch initiation of Caspian and Common Terns at Lake Winnipeg. *Blue Jay* 30:218–220.

Vermeer, K. 1973. Some aspects of the breeding and mortality of Common Loons in East Central Alberta. *Can. Field Nat.* 87:403–408.

Vermeer, K. 1973. Food habits and breeding range of Herring Gulls in the Canadian prairie provinces. *Condor* 75:478–480.

Vermeer, K. 1973. Comparison of egg-laying chronology of Herring and Ring-billed Gulls at Kawinaw Lake. *Can. Field Nat.* 87:306–308.

Vermeer, K. 1973. Great Blue Heron and Double-crested Cormorant colonies in the prairie provinces. *Can. Field Nat.* 87:427–432.

Vermeer, K. F.A.J. Armstrong and D.R.M. Hatch. 1973. Mercury in aquatic birds at Clay Lake, Western Ontario. *J. Wildl. Mgmt.* 37:58–61.

Vermeer, K. 1973. Comparison of mercury contamination of Caspian and Common tern eggs at northern Lake Winnipeg. *Can. Field Nat.* 87:305.

Vermeer, K. 1973. Some aspects of the nesting requirements of Common Loons in Alberta. *Wilson Bull.* 85:429–435.

Vermeer, R. and K. Vermeer. 1974. Oil pollution of birds: an abstracted bibliography. Pesticide Section. *Can. Wildl. Serv. Rept.* 29:1–60.

Vermeer, R. and K. Vermeer. 1974. Biological effects of oil pollution on aquatic organisms: a summarized bibliography. Pesticide Section. *Can. Wildl. Serv. Rept.* 30:1–68.

Vermeer, K., R.W. Risebrough, A.L. Spaans and L.M. Reynolds. 1974. Pesticide effects on fishes and birds in rice fields of Surinam, South America. *Environmental Pollution* 7:217–236.

Sugden, L.G., W.J. Thurlow, R.D. Harris and K. Vermeer. 1974. Investigations of mallards overwintering at Calgary, Alberta. *Can. Field Nat.* 88:303–311.

Vermeer, K. and R. Vermeer. 1975. Oil threat to birds on the Canadian west coast. *Can. Field Nat.* 89:278–298.

Vermeer, K. and G. Anweiler. 1975. Oil threat to aquatic birds along the Yukon coast. *Wilson Bull.* 87:467–480.

Vermeer, K. 1976. Colonial auks and eiders as potential indicators of oil pollution. *Marine Poll. Bull.* 9:165–167.

Vermeer, K, 1976. Global murre watch. *Pacific Seabird Group Bulletin* 3:33–35.

Vermeer, K., K.R. Summers and D.S. Bingham. 1976. Birds observed at Triangle Island. *Murrelet* 57:35–42.

Vermeer, K., D.A. Manuwal and D.S. Bingham. 1976. Seabirds and pinnipeds of Sartine Island, Scott Island Group, British Columbia. *Murrelet* 57:14–16.

Vermeer, K. and C.D. Levings. 1977. Populations, biomass and food habits of ducks on the Fraser Delta tidal flats. *Wildfowl* 28:49–60.

Vermeer, K. 1977. Some observations of Arctic Loons, Brandt's Cormorants and Bonaparte's Gulls at Active Pass, British Columbia. *Murrelet* 58:45–47.

Vermeer, K. 1977. Comparison of White Pelicans from two colonies east and west of the Canadian Rocky Mountains. *Murrelet* 58:79–82.

Vermeer, K. and D.B. Peakall 1977. Toxic chemicals in Canadian fish-eating birds. *Marine Poll. Bull.* 8:205–210.

Vermeer, K. and D.B. Peakall. 1977. Environmental contaminants and the future of fish-eating birds in Canada. Can. Nat. Symp. 88–95.

Vermeer, K. and B.D. Davies. 1978. Comparison of the breeding of Canada and Snow Geese, Westham Island. *Wildfowl* 29:31–43.

Vermeer, K. 1978. Recent reproductive failure of Rhinoceros Auklets and Tufted puffins, British Columbia. *Ibis* 120:112.

Ohlendorff, H.M., R.W. Risebrough and K. Vermeer. 1978. Exposure of marine birds to environmental pollutants. *U.S. Dept. Int. Fish and Wildlife s Report* 3:1–40.

Vermeer, K. and L. Cullen. 1979. Growth of Rhinoceros Auklets and Tufted Puffins, Triangle Island, British Columbia. *Ardea* 67:22–27.

Vermeer, K., L. Cullen and M. Porter. 1979. A provisional explanation of the reproductive failure of Tufted Puffins, Triangle Island, British Columbia. *Ibis* 121:348–354.

Vermeer, K., R.A. Vermeer, K.R. Summers and R.R. Billings. 1979. Numbers and habitat selection of Cassin's Auklets breeding on Triangle Island, British Columbia. *The Auk* 96:143–151.

Vermeer, K. and D.B. Peakall. 1979. Trace metals in seaducks of the Fraser River Delta intertidal area. *Marine Poll. Bull.* 10:189–193.

Vermeer, K. 1980. The importance of timing and type of prey to reproductive success of Rhinoceros Auklets, Cerorhinca monocerata. *Ibis* 122:343–350.

Vermeer, K. 1980. Nesting requirements, food and breeding distribution of Rhinoceros Auklets, *Cerorhinca monocerata,*, and Tufted Puffins, *Lunda cirrhata*. *Ardea* 67:101–110.

Vermeer, K. 1981. Food and populations of Surf Scoters in British Columbia. *Wildfowl* 32:107–116.

Vermeer, K. 1981. The importance of plankton to Cassin's Auklets during breeding. *J. Plank. Res.* 3:315–329.

Vermeer, K. 1982. Food and distribution of three *Bucephala* species in British Columbia waters. *Wildfowl* 33:22–30.

Vermeer, K. 1982. Comparison of the diet of the Glaucous-winged Gull on the east and west coasts of Vancouver Island. *Murrelet* 63:80–85.

Vermeer, K. 1982. Growth comparison of a plankton- and a fish-feeding alcid. *Murrelet* 63:34–39.

Vermeer, K. 1983. Marine bird populations in the Strait of Georgia: comparison with the west coast of Vancouver Island. *Can. Tech. Rep. Hydrogr. Ocean Sci.* No. 19. 18pp.

Vermeer, K., I. Robertson, R.W. Campbell, G. Kaiser and M. Lemon. 1983. Distribution and densities of marine birds on the

Canadian west coast. *Can. Wildl. Serv. Rep.*, Vancouver, British Columbia. 73pp.

Vermeer, K. 1983. Diet of the Harlequin Duck in the Strait of Georgia, British Columbia. *Murrelet* 64:54–57.

Vermeer, K. and N. Bourne. 1984. The White-winged Scoter diet in British Columbia waters; resource partitioning with other scoters, Pp. 30-38. In: Nettleship, D.N., S.G. Sanger and P.F. Springer (Eds.). Marine birds: their feeding ecology and commercial fisheries relationships. *Can. Wildl. Serv. Spec. Publ.*, Ottawa.

Vermeer, K. and S.J. Westerheim. 1984. Fish changes in the Rhinoceros Auklet diet and their implications. Pp. 96–105. In: Nettleship, D.N., S.G. Sanger and P.F. Springer (Eds.). Marine birds: their feeding ecology and commercial fisheries relationships. *Can. Wildl. Serv. Spec. Publ.*, Ottawa.

Vermeer, K. and S.G. Sealy. 1984. Status of nesting seabirds in British Columbia. Pp. 29–40. In Croxall, J.P., P.G.H. Evans and R.W. Schreiber (Eds.). Status and conservation of the world's seabirds. *ICB Tech. Publ.* No. 2. Cambridge.

Vermeer, K. and L. Rankin. 1984. Influence of habitat destruction and disturbance on nesting seabirds. Pp.723–736. In: Croxall, J.P., P.G.H. Evans and R.W. Schreiber (Eds.). Status and conservation of the world's seabirds. *ICBP Tech. Publ.* No. 2. Cambridge.

Vermeer, K., S.G. Sealy, M. Lemon and M. Rodway. 1984. Predation and potential environmental perturbances on Ancient Murrelets nesting in British Columbia. Pp. 757–770. In: Croxall, J.P., P.G.H. Evans and R.W. Schreiber (Eds.). Status and conservation of the world's seabirds. *ICBP Tech. Publ.* No. 2. Cambridge.

Vermeer, K. 1984. The diet and food consumption of nesting Cassin's Auklets during summer and a comparison with other plankton-feeding alcids. *Murrelet* 65:65–77.

Vermeer, K. and L. Rankin. 1984. Population trends in nesting Double-crested and Pelagic cormorants in Canada. *Murrelet* 65:1–9.

Vermeer, K. and L. Rankin. 1984. Pelagic seabird populations in Hecate Strait and Queen Charlotte Sound: comparison with the west coast of the Queen Charlotte Islands. *Can. Tech. Rep. Hydrogr. Ocean Sci.* 52: 1–40.

Vermeer, K. 1985. A five-year summary (1978–1982) of the nestling diet of Cassin's Auklets in British Columbia. *Can. Tech. Rep. Hydrogr. Ocean Sci.* 56:1–15.

Vermeer, K. and L. Rankin. 1985. Pelagic seabird population in Dixon Entrance. *Can. Tech. Rep. Hydrogr. Ocean Sci.* 65:1–22.

Vermeer, K., J.B. Fulton and S.G, Sealy. 1985. Differential use of zooplankton prey by Ancient Murrelets and Cassin's Auklets in the Queen Charlotte Islands. *J. Plank. Res.* 7:443–459.

Vermeer, K. and K. Devito. 1986. Size, caloric content, and association of prey fishes in meals of nestling Rhinoceros Auklets. *Murrelet* 67:1–9.

Vermeer, K. and M. Lemon. 1986. Nesting habits of Ancient Murrelets and Cassin's Auklets in the Queen Charlotte Islands, British Columbia. *Murrelet* 57:33–44.

Vermeer, K., S.G. Sealy and G.A. Sanger. 1987. Feeding ecology of the Alcidae in the eastern North Pacific Ocean. Pp.189–227. In: Croxall, J.P. (Ed.). Seabirds feeding ecology and role in marine ecosystems. Cambridge University Press, Cambridge.

Vermeer, K. and K. Devito. 1987. The importance of *Paracallisoma coecus* and myctophid fishes to nesting Fork-tailed and Leach's Storm-petrels in the Queen Charlotte Islands, British Columbia. *J. Plank. Res.* 10:63–75.

Vermeer, K. and K. Devito. 1987. Habitat and nest-site selection of Mew and Glaucous-winged Gulls in coastal British Columbia. Pp.

105–118. In: J.L. Hand, W.E. Southern, and **K. Vermeer** (Eds.). Ecology and behaviour of gulls. Studies in Avian Biology 10.

Vermeer, K. and K. Devito. 1987. The nesting biology of Mew Gulls (*Larus canus*) on Kennedy Lake, British Columbia, in comparison with Mew Gulls in northern Europe. *Colonial Waterbirds* 9:95–103.

Vermeer, K., I. Szabo and P. Greisman. 1987. The relationship between plankton-feeding Bonaparte's and Mew gulls and tidal upwelling at Active Pass, British Columbia. *J. Plank. Res.* 9:483–501.

Vermeer, K. 1987. Growth and nestling periods of Cassin's Auklets: Adaptations of planktivorous auklets to breeding at northern latitudes. *Can. Tech. Rep. Ocean Sci.* 53:1–26.

Vermeer, K., R. Hay and L. Rankin. 1987. Pelagic seabird populations off southwestern Vancouver Island. *Can. Tech. Rep. Ocean Sci.* 87:1–26.

Hooper, T.D., **K. Vermeer** and I. Szabo. 1987. Oil pollution of birds: an annotated bibliography. *Can. Wildl. Serv. Tech. Rep. Ser.* 34. 180pp.

Hand, J.L., W.E. Southern and **K. Vermeer** (Eds.). 1987. Ecology and behaviour of gulls. Studies in Avian Biology 10. 140pp.

Morgan, K.H., R. Hay and **K. Vermeer**. 1987. Seasonality and distribution of marine birds in Saanich Inlet, Vancouver Island, B.C. Can. Tech. Rep. Hydrogr. *Ocean Sci.* 95: 1–53.

Vermeer, K., K. Devito and L. Rankin. 1988. Comparison of nesting biology of Fork-tailed and Leach's Storm-petrels. *Colonial Waterbirds* 11:46–57.

Vermeer, K., D. Power and G.E.J. Smith. 1988. Habitat selection and nesting biology of roof-nesting Glaucous-winged Gulls. *Colonial Waterbirds* 11:189–201.

Vermeer, K. and R.W. Butler (Eds.). 1989. The ecology and status of marine and shoreline birds of the Strait of Georgia, British Columbia. *Can. Wildl. Serv. Spec. Publ.*, Ottawa. 186pp.

Vermeer, K. 1989. Introduction to the nesting seabirds of the Strait of Georgia. Pp.84–87. In: **Vermeer, K.** and R.W. Butler (Eds.). The ecology and status of marine and shoreline birds of the Strait of Georgia, British Columbia. *Can. Wildl. Serv. Spec. Publ.*, Ottawa.

Vermeer, K. 1989. Marine birds of Jervis Inlet: a mainland fjord entering the Strait of Georgia. Pp. 148–157. In: **Vermeer, K.** and R.W. Butler (Eds.). The ecology and status of marine and shoreline birds of the Strait of Georgia, British Columbia. *Can. Wildl. Serv. Spec. Publ.*, Ottawa.

Vermeer, K. and K.H. Morgan. 1989. Mariculture and bird interactions in the Strait of Georgia. Pp. 174–176. In: **Vermeer, K.** and R.W. Butler (Eds.). The ecology and status of marine and shoreline birds of the Strait of Georgia, British Columbia. *Can. Wildl. Serv. Spec. Publ.*, Ottawa.

Vermeer, K., K.H. Morgan, R.W. Butler and G.E.J. Smith. 1989. Population, nesting habitat and food of Bald Eagles in the Gulf Islands. Pp. 123–130. In: **Vermeer, K.** and R.W. Butler (Eds.). The ecology and status of marine and shoreline birds of the Strait of Georgia, British Columbia. *Can. Wildl. Serv. Spec. Publ.*, Ottawa.

Vermeer, K. and K. Devito. 1989. Population trends of nesting Glaucous-winged Gulls in the Strait of Georgia. Pp. 88–93. In: **Vermeer, K.** and R.W. Butler (Eds.). The ecology and status of marine and shoreline birds of the Strait of Georgia, British Columbia. *Can. Wildl. Serv. Spec. Publ.*, Ottawa.

Vermeer, K., K.H. Morgan and G.E.J. Smith. 1989. Population trends and nesting habitat of Double-crested and Pelagic cormorants in the Strait of Georgia. Pp.94–99. In: **Vermeer, K.** and R.W. Butler (Eds.). The ecology and status of marine and shoreline birds of the Strait of Georgia, British Columbia. *Can. Wildl. Serv. Spec. Publ.*, Ottawa.

Vermeer, K., K.H. Morgan and G.E.J. Smith. 1989. Population and nesting habitat of American Black Oystercatchers in the Strait of

Georgia. Pp. 118–122. In: **Vermeer, K.** and R.W. Butler (Eds.). The ecology and status of marine and shoreline birds of the Strait of Georgia, British Columbia. *Can. Wildl. Serv. Spec. Publ.*, Ottawa.

Vermeer, K. and R. Ydenberg. 1989. Feeding ecology of marine birds in the Strait of Georgia. Pp.62–73. In: **Vermeer, K.** and R.W. Butler (Eds.). The ecology and status of marine and shoreline birds of the Strait of Georgia, British Columbia. *Can. Wildl. Serv. Spec. Publ.*, Ottawa.

Butler, R.W. and **K. Vermeer**. 1989. Overview and recommendations: Important bird habitats and the need for their preservation. Pp. 185–186. In: **Vermeer, K.** and R.W. Butler (Eds.). The ecology and status of marine and shoreline birds of the Strait of Georgia, British Columbia. *Can. Wildl. Serv. Spec. Publ.*, Ottawa.

Vermeer, K, K.H. Morgan, G.E.J. Smith and R. Hay. 1989. Fall distribution of pelagic birds over the shelf off SW Vancouver Island. *Colonial Waterbirds* 12:207–214.

Vermeer, K. 1989. Trace metals in the marine bird food chain downstream from the El Salvador copper mine, Chile. Tech. Rep. Ser. No. 83. *Can. Wildl. Serv.*, British Columbia.

Vermeer, K. and K.H. Morgan. 1989. Nesting population, nest sites, and prey remains of Bald Eagles in Barkley Sound, British Columbia. *Northwestern Naturalist* 70:21–26.

Vermeer, K. and J.C. Castilla. 1991. High cadmium residues observed in a pilot study in shorebirds and their prey downstream from the El Salvador Copper Mine, Chile. *Bull. Environ. Contam. Toxicol.* 46:242–248.

Vermeer, K., K.H. Morgan, G.E.J. Smith and B.A. York. 1991. Effects of egging on the reproductive success of Glaucous-winged Gulls. *Colonial Waterbirds* 14:158–165.

Whitehead, P.E., J.E. Elliott, R.J. Norstrom and **K. Vermeer**. 1991. PCDD and PCDF contamination of waterfowl in the Strait of Georgia, British Columbia, Canada 1969–1990. *Proceedings Dioxin* 1990. 1:459–463.

Vermeer, K., K.H. Morgan, M. Bentley, F. Goodfellow and N. Beatty. 1991. The importance of spring staging areas of Brant (*Branta bernicla*) and the distribution of other marine birds near Sandspit, Queen Charlotte Islands. *Tech. Rep.* Ser. No. 136. Canadian Wildlife Service, British Columbia.

Vermeer, K. and D.B. Irons. 1991. The Glaucous-winged Gull on the Pacific coast of North America. *Proc. 20th Int. Orn. Congr.* 2378–2383.

Morgan, K.H., **K. Vermeer** and R.W. McKelvey. 1991. Atlas of pelagic birds of western Canada. Occasional Paper No. 72. Canadian Wildlife Service, Ottawa.

Vermeer, K. and J.A.J. Thompson. 1992. Arsenic and copper residues in waterbirds and their food down inlet from the Island Copper Mill. *Bull. Environ. Contam. Toxicol.* 48:733–738.

Vermeer, K., K.H. Morgan and G.E.J. Smith. 1992. Black Oystercatcher habitat selection, reproductive success, and their relationship with Glaucous-winged Gulls. *Colonial Waterbirds* 15:14–23.

Vermeer, K. 1992. Population growth of the Glaucous-winged Gull (*Larus glaucescens*) in the Strait of Georgia, British Columbia, Canada. *Ardea* 80:181–185.

Vermeer, K., R.W. Butler and K.H. Morgan (Eds.). 1992. The ecology, status, and conservation of marine and shoreline birds on the west coast of Vancouver Island. *Occ. Paper No. 75*, Canadian Wildlife Service, Ottawa, 136 pp.

Vermeer, K. 1992. The diet of birds as a tool for monitoring the biological environment. Pp. 41–50 In: **Vermeer, K.**, R.W. Butler and K.H.

Morgan (Eds.). The ecology status and conservation of marine and shoreline birds on the west coast of Vancouver Island. *Occ. Paper No. 75*. Canadian Wildlife Service, Ottawa.

Vermeer, K., K.H..Morgan and P.J. Ewins. 1992. Population trends of Pelagic Cormorants and Glaucous-winged Gulls nesting on the west coast of Vancouver Island. Pp. 60–64. In: **Vermeer, K.**, R.W. Butler and K.H. Morgan (Eds.). The ecology, status and conservation of marine and shoreline birds on the west coast of Vancouver Island. *Occ. Paper No. 75*. Canadian Wildlife Service, Ottawa.

Vermeer, K., P.J. Ewins, K.H. Morgan and G.E.J. Smith. 1992. Population, nesting habitat, and reproductive success of American Black Oystercatchers on the west coast of Vancouver Island. Pp. 55–70. In: **Vermeer, K.**, R.W. Butler and K.H. Morgan (Eds.). The ecology, status and conservation of marine and shoreline birds on the west coast of Vancouver Island. *Occ. Paper No. 75*. Canadian Wildlife Service, Ottawa.

Vermeer, K., K.H. Morgan and G.E.J. Smith. 1992. Habitat analysis of co-occurrence of seabirds on the west coast of Vancouver Island. Pp. 78–85. In: **Vermeer, K.**, R.W. Butler and K.H. Morgan (Eds.). The ecology, status and conservation of marine and shoreline birds on the west coast of Vancouver Island. *Occ. Paper No. 75*. Canadian Wildlife Service, Ottawa.

Vermeer, K. and K.H. Morgan.1992. Marine bird populations and habitat use in a fjord on the west coast of Vancouver Island. Pp.86–96. In: **Vermeer, K.**, R.W. Butler and K.H. Morgan (Eds.). The ecology, status and conservation of marine and shoreline birds on the west coast of Vancouver Island. *Occ. Paper No. 75*. Canadian Wildlife Service, Ottawa.

Vermeer, K., K.H. Morgan, A. Dorst and B. Whittington. 1992. Bird populations of estuaries on the southwest coast of Vancouver Island. Pp.97–108. In: **Vermeer, K.**, R.W. Butler and K.H. Morgan (Eds.). The ecology, status and conservation of marine and shoreline birds on the west coast of Vancouver Island. *Occ. Paper No. 75.* Canadian Wildlife Service, Ottawa.

Morgan, K.H., R.W. Butler and **K. Vermeer**. 1992. Environmental disturbance and conservation of marine and shoreline birds on the west coast of Vancouver Island. Pp.129–132. In: **Vermeer, K.**, R.W. Butler and K.H. Morgan (Eds.). The ecology, status and conservation of marine and shoreline birds on the west coast of Vancouver Island. *Occ. Paper No. 75.* Canadian Wildlife Service, Ottawa.

Vermeer, K., K.T. Briggs, K.H. Morgan and D. Siegel-Causey. (Eds.) 1993. The status, ecology and conservation of marine birds of the North Pacific. *Can. Wildl. Serv. Spec. Publ.* Ottawa, 263 pp.

Vermeer, K., D.B. Irons, E. Velarde, and Y. Watanuki. 1993. Status, conservation and management of nesting Larus gulls in the North Pacific. Pp. 131–139. In: **Vermeer, K.**, K.T. Briggs, K.H. Morgan and D. Siegel-Causey (Eds.). The status, ecology and conservation of marine birds of the North Pacific. *Can. Wildl. Serv. Spec. Publ.* Ottawa.

Wahl, T.R., K.H. Morgan and **K. Vermeer**. 1993. Seabird distribution of British Columbia and Washington. Pp. 39–47. In: **Vermeer, K.**, K.T. Briggs, K.H. Morgan and D. Siegel-Causey (Eds.). The status, ecology and conservation of marine birds of the North Pacific. *Can. Wildl. Serv. Spec. Publ.* Ottawa.

Vermeer, K., K.H. Morgan and G.E.J. Smith. 1993. Colony attendance of Pigeon Guillemots as related to tide height and time of day. *Colonial Waterbirds* 16:1–8.

Vermeer, K., K.H. Morgan and G.E.J. Smith. 1993. Nesting biology and predation of Pigeon Guillemots in the Queen Charlotte Islands, British Columbia. *Colonial Waterbirds* 16:119–127.

Vermeer, K., W.J. Cretney, J.E. Elliott, R.J. Norstrom and P.E. Whitehead. 1993. Elevated polychlorinated dibenzodioxins and dibenzofuran concentrations in grebes, ducks and their prey near Port Alberni, British Columbia, Canada. *Mar. Pollution Bull.* 26:431–435.

Mahaffy, M.S., D.R. Nysewander, **K. Vermeer**, T.R. Wahl and P.E. Whitehead.1994. Status, trends and potential threats related to birds in the Strait of Georgia. Pp. 256–281. In: Wilson, R.C.H., R.J. Beamish, F. Aitkens and J. Bell (Eds.). Review of the marine environment and biota of Strait of Georgia, Puget Sound and Juan de Fuca Strait. *Can. Tech. Rep. Fish Aqua. Sci.* No. 1948.

Goudie, R.I., S. Brault, B. Conant, A.V. Kondratyev, M.R. Peterson and **K. Vermeer**. 1994. The status of sea ducks in the North Pacific Rim: toward their conservation and management. In: Conserving International Resources of the North Pacific Rim. 59th North American Wildlife and Natural Resources Conference, Anchorage, Alaska.

Ewins, P.J., K.H. Morgan and **K. Vermeer**. 1994. The distribution of Pigeon Guillemots (*Cepphus columba*) breeding on the west coast of Vancouver Island, British Columbia, in 1989. Northwestern Naturalist. In press.

Vermeer, K. 1994. Population trends of nesting marine birds in the Strait of Georgia and on the west coast of Vancouver Island. Pacific Ecozone Workshop, February 1–3, 1994, Institute of Ocean Sciences, Sidney, B.C. In press.

Butler, R.W. and **K. Vermeer** (Eds.) 1994. The abundance and distribution of estuarine birds in the Strait of Georgia, British Columbia. *Can. Wildl. Serv. Occ. Paper* No. 83, Ottawa, 78 pp.

Vermeer, K., R.W. Butler and K.H. Morgan. 1994. Comparison of seasonal shorebird and waterbird densities within Fraser River delta intertidal regions. Pp. 6–17. In: R.W. Butler and **K. Vermeer** (Eds.). The abundance and distribution of estuarine birds in the Strait of Georgia, British Columbia. *Can. Wildl. Serv. Occ. Paper* No. 83, Ottawa.

Vermeer, K. 1994. Seasonal changes in waterbird composition and population of the Gorge, an urban estuary. Pp.37–48. In: R.W. Butler and **K. Vermeer** (Eds.). The abundance and distribution of estuarine birds in the Strait of Georgia, British Columbia. *Can. Wildl. Serv. Occ. Paper* No. 83, Ottawa.

Vermeer, K., M. Bentley and K.H. Morgan. 1994. Comparison of waterbird populations in the Chemainus, Cowichan and Nanaimo river estuaries. Pp. 44–56. In: R.W. Butler and **K. Vermeer** (Eds.). The abundance and distribution of estuarine birds in the Strait of Georgia, British Columbia. *Can. Wildl. Serv. Occ. Paper* No. 83, Ottawa.

Vermeer, K. 1994. Waterbird populations in the Courtenay River estuary: A comparison with southern Vancouver Island estuaries. Pp. 57–62. In: R.W. Butler and **K. Vermeer** (Eds.). The abundance and distribution of estuarine birds in the Strait of Georgia, British Columbia. *Can. Wildl. Serv. Occ. Paper* No. 83, Ottawa.

Vermeer, K., K.H. Morgan, G.E.J. Smith and A.N. Wisely. 1994. Habitat use by waterbirds in the Cowichan River estuary. Pp 63-69. In: R.W. Butler and **K. Vermeer** (Eds.). The abundance and distribution of estuarine birds in the Strait of Georgia, British Columbia. *Can. Wildl. Serv. Occ. Paper* No. 83, Ottawa.

Butler, R.W., **K. Vermeer** and G.E.J. Smith. 1994. Estimated energy consumption by estuarine birds at different trophic levels. Pp. 70–74. In: R.W. Butler and **K. Vermeer** (Eds.). The abundance and distribution of estuarine birds in the Strait of Georgia, British Columbia. *Can. Wildl. Serv. Occ. Paper* No. 83, Ottawa.

Vermeer, K. and R.W. Butler. 1994. The international significance and the need for environmental knowledge of estuaries. Pp.75–76. In: R.W. Butler and **K. Vermeer** (Eds.). The abundance and distribution of estuarine birds in the Strait of Georgia, British Columbia. *Can. Wildl. Serv. Occ. Paper* No. 83, Ottawa.

Acknowledgments

My wife Rebecca encouraged and supported me through all stages of writing and publishing this book. Tributes by Alan Burger, Robert Butler, and Ron Ydenberg are much appreciated, and add a different perspective to this story. The tributes were published in the program of the Joint Conference of the Colonial Waterbird Society and the Pacific Seabird Group in Victoria, British Columbia on November 8–12, 1995. My university friend, the late Rudi Drent, introduced me to my first study of seabirds on Mandarte Island, which eventually set the stage for my career as a professional ornithologist with the Canadian Wildlife Service. Douglas Bertram, who continues my studies of Cassin's Auklets in British Columbia, shared new information on that species relating to climate variability. Tom Bijvoet, publisher of *Dutch the Magazine* and *Maandblad de krant*, and Annie McLeod, editor of *Nature Saskatchewan's Blue Jay*, endorsed my story with pertinent comments. Nicholas Bowlin, of One Hour Photo in Sidney, edited old photographs. Wally du Temple, a friend since university, introduced me to FriesenPress, where the editor and staff, notably Jessica Feser, provided guidance and support throughout the production and publication of this book. Co-editors, co-authors, assistants, and contractors either assisted or cooperated with the undertaking of biological investigations and projects. Family in Holland commented on some of my early stories. I thank them all.

About the Author

In 1930, Kees Vermeer was born in Noordeloos, a small village in the Dutch polder, where he acquired his first interest in birds and nature. Kees was almost ten when the Nazis invaded Holland, where at one time his family was forced to share their home with a German tank crew. He also witnessed the historic surrender of the German army in his hometown Gorinchem. In 1954, Kees immigrated to Canada, where after a few months of farming, he accepted any jobs available to him until he realized he needed more education. He enrolled at the University of British Columbia (BC) in 1956, where he obtained a Bachelor of Science degree in Geology and Zoology in 1959, and a Master of Science degree in Zoology in 1963. For his Master thesis, he studied the nesting biology of Glaucous-winged Gulls on Mandarte Island, a small rocky islet near Sidney along the BC coast. Even though his thesis was published in an obscure provincial museum series, it became a Citation Classic. Kees completed his doctorate in Zoology at the University of Alberta in 1967. As a research scientist for the Government of Canada, Kees studied the ecology of fresh water and marine bird populations. He also investigated the effects of changes in seawater temperatures; that of pesticides, mercury and oil pollution; and habitat destruction and predation on aquatic birds. Kees presently lives with his wife Rebecca in North Saanich on Vancouver Island, British Columbia. In his retirement, he enjoys bird watching, gardening, history and travel. In his eighties, he began writing short stories for his family in the Netherlands, which eventually culminated in his autobiography, *Immigrant Gone to Heaven*.

CPSIA information can be obtained
at www.ICGtesting.com
Printed in the USA
BVHW060809121221
623753BV00003B/9